YOU TOO CAN

DISCOVER

THE FOUNTAIN

OF YOUTH

by Archie Phillips

ISBN 0-936513-25-X

Library of Congress 98-075012

Published by Larsen's Outdoor Publishing

Distributed by
Archie Phillips
P. O. Box 377
Fairfield, AL 35064
(205)787-6902

PRINTED IN THE UNITED STATES OF AMERICA

1 2 3 4 5

NOTE TO READERS

The information contained in this book is given for the purpose of teaching the readers a healthy lifestyle. It is not intended as a substitute for the medical advice of physicians. The readers should regularly consult their doctors if they have a medical problem or symptoms that may require diagnosis. Nutritional needs vary from person to person, depending on age, sex, health status, and total diet.

ACKNOWLEDGMENTS

I couldn't have written this book or become interested in learning about good health without the help of my friends who inspired and encouraged me, Dr. Marshall Ringsdorf, Jr., and Dr. Klyde Albritton, both of Birmingham, Alabama. Their guidance and suggestions of books to read and information for me to study helped me put myself on the path to rediscover the fountain of youth. Dr. Gus Prosch of Birmingham also made me aware of the values of chelation therapy.

I also appreciate the recommendations my sister-in-law Denise Phillips made to make the book more interesting. And I'm very proud to have the cartoons of Charles G. Brooks, the editorial cartoonist for The Birminghan News for 38 years, to illustrate my book. I've known Charles for many years and always have admired his art. Charles' cartoons are in permanent collections at the Harry S. Truman Library, the Sam Rayburn Library, the FBI, the Library of Congress and the Dwight D. Eisenhower Museum to name a few and have been featured in more than 80 books. A former WWII veteran who participated in D-Day and the Battle of the Bulge, Charles has received 13 Freedom Foundation awards, two Vigilant Patriot Awards and the national Sigma Delta Chi Award for Editorial Cartooning during his career.

I also want to thank Larry and Lilliam Larsen at Larsen's Outdoor Publishing in Lakeland, Florida, who took my words and research and Charles' cartoons and put them in a readable form for you to learn from, refer back to and enjoy.

CONTENTS

FOREWORD

"This book is for anyone who wants to get well and/or stay well. It describes a nutrition program that will help the reader eat right, lose weight, and stay healthy. It also emphasizes the importance of exercise in disease prevention and weight control.

"The author stresses the importance of eating a king's breakfast, a prince's lunch and a pauper's supper. He maintains that skipping breakfast is a slow way of self-destruction. Doris (my wife) and I have been eating the breakfast described in this book for almost six months. We highly recommend it as a good way to start the day.

"This book gives ample evidence of the nutritional inadequacy of the average American's diet and advises the replacement of lost nutrients with food supplements. It also effectively points out the health pitfalls from consumption of refined sugar, refined flour, caffeine, saturated fat, salt and red meat. The harmful health effects of other bad lifestyles are also discussed: smoking, alcohol consumption and the chemicals in our food, air, and water.

"This book describes and explains some heavy scientific data in a light and interesting manner. The reader will not be bored. Cartoon illustrations are placed at strategic places throughout this book to clarify discussions in the text. Readers should get another copy for a family member or friend."

W. Marshall Ringsdorf, Jr., D. M. D.
728 Sussex Drive, Birmingham, Alabama 35226
(205) 822-7679

Warren Marshall Ringsdorf, Jr. is the author and co-author of numerous books including Diet & Disease, Diet & the Periodontal Patient, New Hope for Incurable Diseases, Psychadietetics, a best seller, having seven hardcover editions, and The Vitamin C Connection.

He also has written 400 articles for various professional journals of medicine, dentistry and other health science fields.

Born in Elba, Alabama, Dr. Ringsdorf studied at the University of Alabama School of Dentistry, earning his DMD in 1956. He also obtained his MS degree in 1956 from the University of Alabama Graduate School in Tuscaloosa. Besides having a dental practice, he has been an assistant professor of Clinical Dentistry in the departments of Oral Medicine and Oral Diagnosis at the University of Alabama School of Dentistry in Birmingham, Alabama. The recipient of many awards and honors, Dr. Ringsdorf's accomplishments appear in numerous biographical listings, including "Notable Americans," "Who's Who in the South & Southwest," "American Men & Women of Science," "Who's Who in Health Care," "Men & Women of Distinction," "Men of Achievement," "Two Thousand Notable Americans," "The International Who's-Who of Intellectuals," and "Community Leaders of the World."

Dr. Ringsdorf's main field of interest is diet and nutrition and the application of this to health maintenance and recovery. He conducts a practice in nutritional and lifestyle counseling.

INTRODUCTION

Hi Folks!

I'm Archie Phillips. You may have seen my TV show. For the last 10 years I have been the host of *Outdoors With Archie Phillips*. I've done episodes of hunting and fishing all over the country.

You probably remember me as a good hefty 230 pounds on my five foot eight-and-a-half inch frame. I had a 46-inch waist, and I enjoyed my hunting and fishing and my family as much as anybody.

Of course, I had a little more trouble getting in and out of the boat, walking around in the woods chasing rabbits and doing other active things when I was that heavy. I didn't know that I was having trouble because I'd been overweight all my adult life.

To save my life, I came from a 46-inch waist down to a 32-inch waist. In the process, I discovered some very new and interesting ideas on how to take weight off in a nutritionally sound manner. I wrote this book because I wanted to share what I learned with you. I also made a video that you could watch to help you realize the importance of caring enough about your health to do something about it.

A LITTLE KNOT LEADS TO A BIG DISCOVERY

You can see in my picture just how much weight I was carrying around, and I didn't think anything about it. I thought I was doing fine. Everything was lovely until one day I decided to let my doctor look at a little knot that had come up on the top of my head.

The knot wasn't unusual. I had one come up before that was just a little sebaceous cyst. It's where a hair turns down and makes a little bump.

I went to my medical doctor, thinking my cyst just needed a real simple operation. I figured the doctor would take a razor and shave a little hair off. Then he might use a scalpel to cut a little slit and pull out this little cyst and it's all over. You're talking about a very minor operation.

So I wasn't prepared for all the fuss. I went to my doctor who checked my tongue, my ears and everything, and then he said the cyst wasn't his specialty.

I said, "Look doc, all I want you to do is just cut the little bump out of my head. I don't need to go through all this." But he referred me to another doctor.

I went to that doctor and he said, "Yeah, there shouldn't be any problem, but we've got to run all these tests."

I said, "Doc, I have just got through running all those tests." But he told me that we were going to do it again."

Oh, me. I felt like an old log in one of those logging chutes. You know, the old timers used to put a log in there and float it down into the river. There I was. I was in the "system."

I said, "OK, go ahead and do it."

So the first thing he said was, "Go in the rest room there. I need a urine sample in this little jar."

I said, "OK." Boy, by then I was vexed! Going through all this business just to get a little knot cut out of the top of my head.

TROUBLE WITH HIGH BLOOD SUGAR

I was back conferring with the doctor in his office when the nurse came in and said, "Doc, he's got sugar in his urine and quite a bit of it."

The Doc says, "OK. Get your arm out here and give me some blood."

So I put my arm out, and the nurse took some blood. The test came back that I had a 330 milligrams blood sugar count. The top side of normal is 150 milligrams of sugar per 100 milliliters of blood.

"Friend, you're about ready for a needle of insulin. Diabetic," he said. "You're a diabetic."

I said, "Doc, I ain't no diabetic."

"Yeah, you are," he said. "Anybody is who has that much blood sugar. Now you've got two or three choices. First we can try you on some of these pills and see how they work. You need to take some of this weight off and this, that, and the other." I was overwhelmed.

But to make it more complicated, this particular doctor was also the doctor who gave medical tests for people to keep their pilots' licenses. Whenever you fill out a form, one of the questions is, "Are you a pilot?" If you check that "yes," then your medical information isn't privileged. The doctor has to send it straight to the Federal Aviation Administration (FAA).

So, the FAA suspended my flying license when this condition was discovered. I got a big, long letter from the FAA that said, "Mr. Phillips, you will submit to the following tests." It went on and on and on. In fact it was the same test that a 747 pilot would have to take.

Well, by the time I left the doctor's office, I was depressed and down and just really upset. As I drove home, I was thinking, "What am I going to do now?"

But I'm not the kind of guy who gives up easily. By the time I got home, I decided to call my good friend Dr. W. K. Albritton to see if he could help me. He could and did! He helped me to find the fountain of youth.

Chapter 1

HOW I GOT STARTED ON A HEALTHY DIET

I had one of the biggest shocks in my life a couple of years ago. I went to the doctor thinking I was in good health and found out I had diabetes — bad diabetes. The doctor insisted I had to lose lots of weight. You can understand why I left the doctor's office very upset and depressed.

Although I had been overweight all my life, I enjoyed good health — or so I thought. I've always had an active life and still could keep up with the rest of my hunting and fishing buddies who were 20 or 30 years younger then me.

I have a successful taxidermy business. I've also published several books and have a long running hunting and fishing syndicated TV show, *Outdoors with Archie Phillips.*

I'm a happy person and feel very lucky. My wife and my son work with me in my businesses.

Until the day I found out I had diabetes, I never thought about my health. Like most people, I just took my health for granted. When I returned home from the doctor's office that day, I called a deer hunting and fishing friend who's knowledgeable about good nutrition. Dr. W. K. Albritton of Birmingham, Alabama, is a retired, 76-year old dentist who looks and acts 20 years younger. Albritton scuba dives with me. I never have helped him put on his diving gear. He can walk all day in the woods and stay at pace with most anyone.

But when Dr. Albritton was about 45, he was diagnosed with cancer. He set out to learn everything he could about health and food. Today he has no sign of the cancer.

With his medical education as a background, Klyde studied the available information on medicine, nutrition and exercise. He worked out a program to improve his health. He's stuck to it ever since. He's never had any more trouble or been sick again. He is a perfect specimen of healthiness.

Therefore, Klyde was the first person I could think to call when I considered what life would be like if I had to use insulin and carry it with me everywhere I went. I knew if my activity level was high, my blood sugar level would be low. Then I would feel bad.

I was very upset when I called Klyde. When I told Klyde exactly what had happened, he said calmly, "Well, Archie, that's no problem."

"What do you mean I don't have a problem?" I yelled back. I was getting more upset.

"Well, if you'd quit eating all the junk food you do and get on a proper diet, then your body would cure itself," Klyde said quietly. "Unless you've had juvenile diabetes or some problem that has destroyed your pancreas, your pancreas will start functioning properly. Then everything will be fine when you get the proper food and enzymes back in your body."

Somewhat relieved, I asked Klyde to give me a quick seminar to get me underway. Klyde told me if I planned to do this program, I had to comply 100 percent. He was very serious. I told Klyde not to worry, and I'd do whatever he said.

" Your words, Klyde, will be like the words in a prayer book as far as I'm concerned, because I've already struck out eating and living like I have been." Klyde explained he wasn't giving me theories.

He told me "One hundred percent of the time from now on, you can't have ...
* "caffeine of any kind,
* "sugar,
* "bread,
* "red meat or
* "fried foods.
"Is that clear?"

Although Klyde sounded like a drill sergeant, I told him the program sounded fine. Then I asked what kind of meat or protein was I going to eat. He said, "You'll eat ... *
* "chicken,
* "turkey,
* "fish,
* "beans & rice and
* "tofu, and none of it will be fried."

As Klyde warmed to his subject, he said, "If you were a smoker, you'd have to quit today. If you were a drinker, you'd have to keep your alcoholic intake to a low amount. You must exercise regularly, too.

"Remember this fact about food. The Good Lord put the right stuff here for us to eat. But in the process, we've

destroyed most of the good things in food by preservatives, overcooking and overprocessing things before they get to your table.

"For example, if you bruise a fruit or a vegetable, you lose vitamins. The longer the fresh food sits in the warehouse and the store, the more nutrition that is lost. Even if you pick greens out of your garden, which is the best way to get the proper vitamins, you still will lose nutrition if you cook it wrong or too long.

"Meat must be prepared and cooked properly to keep its nutritional value. Processed meat like sandwich meat has a lot of chemicals you don't want to put in your body. Pesticides and other chemicals also are problems."

"Don't worry, plenty of good food still is available for you to eat that's not hard to find. We'll get you on a proper, nutritious food program.

"Now, understand, I didn't use the word diet. I said nutritious food program," his voice boomed into the phone." You'll have to stick with it the rest of your life."

I said without hesitating, "OK. Let's get with it."

Chapter 2

THE NUTRITIOUS PROGRAM

The program Dr. Klyde Albritton gave me is explained here. This way of living set me on a course that not only straightened out my blood sugar but also helped me lose 80 pounds and keep it off.

The key to my success was a change in my attitude about my health. I made up my mind to learn how to become healthy and committed myself to an entirely different way of life. Klyde told me this program was a way of life, not a diet.

I wasn't trying to become thin. I simply wanted my good health back.

If you diet to look better or because you're overweight, then you may not have as much success as some people do. A healthy lifestyle includes good nutrition, exercise and a healthy attitude about life.

Once I'd been on this program for some time, I increased the level of my exercise program because I felt so good. But I continued to have a problem with a large pouch of skin still left around my middle that became ulcerated periodically. I eventually had to have much of this excess skin removed and tucked by a doctor to end my problems. Hopefully faithful exercise would keep you from this type of problem.

THE IMPORTANCE OF BREAKFAST

The description of the food part of the program follows. I personally suggest you reinforce this food program with a quality multi-vitamin, 1000 milligrams of vitamin C, 400

units of vitamin E, a combination of B vitamins in a tablet and a tablet of cod liver oil. Chapter 6 explains how important vitamins are to good health. Chapter 4 tells the importance of exercise. The dangers of fat and sugar are found in Chapters 10 and 11.

"Breakfast is the most important meal you'll eat all day," Dr. Albritton began. "Folks who don't eat breakfast are committing suicide. Eat breakfast like a king, lunch like a prince and dinner like a pauper to be healthy."

THE KING'S FEAST

I use a quart-size plastic bowl for my breakfast. According to Dr. Albritton, everything that goes into the bowl has a purpose.

BREAKFAST:

1/4-cup Old Fashioned Quaker Oats, uncooked
1/4-cup wheat germ
1 small banana or 1/2-large one cut-up

2 tablespoons raisins or half of a 1-1/2-ounce box of raisins

12 red, seedless grapes

1 small or 1/2-large red apple cut-up

1/2-cup of berries (strawberries, blueberries)

1 slice fresh pineapple cut up (optional)

6 ounces skim milk

sugar substitute to sweeten to taste (optional)

You can buy wheat germ and the oats at the grocery store. One-fourth cup of wheat germ helps your system get the proper amount of vitamin B each day. Many people put wheat germ on salads and mix it in other things. However, remember that once you open the lid, wheat germ oxidizes quickly. Put wheat germ immediately in the refrigerator. Don't leave it sitting around.

The 6 ounces of skim milk is important to your health. Don't even use 2 percent milk, because skim is half of 1 percent milk fat. If you can't drink milk, just use a small amount. A banana is a stable, nutritious food that has numbers of enzymes, potassium and vitamins to build your health. A banana also has the correct amount of starches. You probably won't need the sweetener because the fruit is sweet.

The expression "an apple a day keeps the doctor away" is true. An apple is full of enzymes, vitamins and fiber to make your body work properly. I particularly like the small Rome apples. Some folks prefer Delicious apples. Especially in the fall, you'll have a huge variety of apples from which to choose.

The sliced pineapple is optional and available at many grocery stores already sliced. Some stores will cut the pineapple for you. Then you know the pineapple is fresh. Don't use canned anything — only fresh.

The raisins, grapes, berries, milk, oats and the other ingredients all add up to a nutritious breakfast full of vitamins, minerals, enzymes, protein and fiber. Every single one of these foods is something the Good Lord has put on this earth with good stuff in it. So use it.

When you see how full the bowl is, you'll think this is a large amount of food. If this big breakfast is too much, cut

BREAKFAST   LUNCH   SUPPER

the volume in half. But don't cut short the amount of oats or wheat germ.

Drink a glass of juice or milk with your bowl full of fruits, oats and wheat germ. Don't drink coffee or a caffeine drink. I talk more about problems caffeine causes in Chapter 5.

Klyde didn't talk to me about calories. This way of eating doesn't count calories like some diets advise. But when you've filled the bowl as I've suggested, you'll be ingesting about 400 calories. I'll talk more about calories later. This delicious and fresh breakfast tastes superb and will get your body going good for the day.

SNACK — 9:30 or 10:00 a.m. Eat one:

Apple, Grapes, Peach, Pear, Orange, Carrot and DRINK WATER.

You must eat several snacks a day to keep your energy level up and your blood sugar level even. Forget what your mother may have taught you about not snacking between meals. Your health will be better when you eat five or six small meals rather than three, large ones. Spoil your dinner with nutritious snacks. Take the edge off your appetite. Then you won't eat so much at once.

Klyde told me, "About 9:30 or 10:00 a.m., I eat an apple, a peach, grapes, a pear or a carrot. Eat a carrot at some time every single day.

"You also need to eat one citrus fruit, preferably a lemon every day. Cut a lemon in half. Squeeze it into a glass of ice water at snack time or lunch. Do the same thing at supper for super-tasting lemonade. Lemons are an important part of this food program."

Drink at least six to eight, 8-ounce glasses of water a day in addition to anything else you drink.

EAT LUNCH LIKE A PRINCE:

Baked, skinless chicken, three vegetables, broiled or baked fish, beans and rice, tofu, or skinless turkey.

Lunch is a simple meal, whether you eat at your local cafeteria or fix it yourself. Eat baked chicken and any three vegetables you choose. Most home-style restaurants serve green beans, carrots, sweet potatoes, spinach, corn, squash, rutabagas, beets, broccoli, turnip greens, collard greens, cabbage and many more vegetables.

Take the skin off the chicken. You'll never eat any chicken skin again. If you are cooking the chicken, take the skin off before you bake it. Chicken skin is full of fat, which will interfere with some of the enzyme action in your body. If you're already overweight like I was, cut down on the amount of fat you eat to reduce the percent of fat in your body. I try to keep fat to only 20 percent of my daily calories. (See Chapter 10 for more on fat).

You'll still get plenty of fat in other foods you can't help. Chicken baked without the skin on still will have some fat. You'll also get some fat when the cook flavors your food.

You will have had a filling lunch, but only 700 calories.

SNACK — 3:30 p.m.: Eat one piece of fruit. Drink water. In the afternoon, eat another piece of fruit. An apple, a peach, a pear or an orange will keep your energy level up much better than a cup of coffee or a cola drink will. Be sure to drink more water.

EAT SUPPER LIKE A PAUPER:

Three ounces of baked chicken, Lettuce, Bell pepper, Tomatoes, Carrots, Other vegetables like onions, etc., Light vinaigrette salad dressing

DON'T EAT A "DOG DIET"— ONE LARGE MEAL AT NIGHT. SPREAD YOUR MEALS OVER 6 OR 8 STOPS TO KEEP YOUR BODY SUGAR IN THE SAFE ZONE... AND YOUR BODY RUNNING SMOOTHLY.

Supper is simple—something like a chicken salad with lettuce like those made by many of the fast-food chains. I like McDonald's Chunky Chicken Salad, which is the size of salad you need to eat for supper.

This salad will contain a total of about 200 calories. You can use fish, turkey or tofu instead of chicken if you prefer.

BEFORE BEDTIME SNACK:

Eat a piece of fruit. Drink more water.

About 20 to 30 minutes before you go to bed, eat a piece of fruit to carry you through the night. Then you won't be hungry during the night. Drink more water, too. To be successful with this food program, feel better and have more energy, you must stick to it.

CALORIES

Let's talk about calories. This food plan gives you about 1,200 to 1,300 calories a day. An adult man 50 to 60 years old burns about 2,200 calories a day, which means a deficit of 700 to 800 calories a day. A woman burns about 300 calories less per day. You must burn 3,500 calories to lose a pound. If you have a 700-calorie deficit over seven days, you'll lose 1-1/2 to 2 pounds every week.

MESSING UP ONCE A WEEK IS O.K.

Once you've been on this diet for a while, you'll be tempted to slack off. Just go ahead, and mess up once a week. Grandma or your boss may invite you to eat. As you know, food is a social function.

Perhaps you go out to eat, and someone serves gravy and rice and salad. Then you say to yourself, "Don't worry. I'll take a break, splurge, and eat all I want."

But what will happen to your weight? After two or three days, your weight will continue to fall. But if you mess up twice a week, you'll be at a maintenance level, and nothing will happen. Any more than twice-a-week mess-ups and you'll be going backwards. Part of this program includes messing up once a week. Go to it! Just keep to the program the rest of the week.

THE PROTEIN FACTOR

Many people try to lose weight by reducing the amount of fat in their diets and eating more carbohydrates. But recent research has indicated that a low-fat, high-carbohydrate diet actually can make you fat!

Here's the reasoning behind this theory. A diet high in carbohydrates sends insulin levels soaring. Your body interprets this signal as a need to store calories, which end up as body fat. Researchers say the solution to this problem is to eat an adequate amount of protein instead of too many carbohydrates. I know many people who have had success with this diet.

If you're interested in learning more about protein, read Protein Power by Michael R. Eades, M.D., and Mary Dan Eades, M.D. (Bantam Books, 1996).

NEW ATTITUDE ABOUT WEIGHT

If you're like me, you may not know what you should weigh at the age you are now. The U.S. government published a new weight scale in 1990 as a part of their Dietary Guidelines for Americans.

For many years the medical community followed the strict 1959 Metropolitan Life table. However, most Americans, especially middle-aged people, weighed much more than the chart said they should. This table also did not allow for stout, thick bones or well-developed muscles.

Men or Women (without shoes or clothes)		
	Age 19-34	35 and up
Height	Weight	Weight
5'0"	97-129	108-138
5'1"	101-132	111-143
5'2"	104-137	115-148
5'3"	107-141	119-152
5'5"	114-150	122-157
5'6"	118-155	130-167
5'7"	121-160	134-172
5'8"	125-164	138-178
5'9"	129-169	142-183
5'10"	132-174	146-188
5'11"	136-179	151-194
6'0"	140-184	155-199
6'1"	144-189	159-205
6'2"	148-195	164-210
6'3"	152-200	168-216
Body Mass Index	19-25	21-27

Even though the chart shown here is more liberal, don't attempt to fill out to fit the top level. Aim for the lower range. Many medical conditions like high-blood pressure and diabetes improve with weight loss. Follow your doctor's advice. Unfortunately, even with using this new table, more than 25 percent of Americans are overweight.

THE SHOPPING LIST

Shop for fresh meat, fish, fruit and vegetables. Read the labels carefully on canned or processed food. Watch carefully for added salt, sugar and fat.

PROTEIN

Chicken, Turkey, Fish, Tofu, Beans, Brown rice

SALAD

Lettuce, Tomatoes, Carrots, Bell pepper, Mild onion

BREAKFAST

Skim milk · 1/2 percent milk fat, Old Fashioned Quaker Oats, Wheat germ, Raisins, Bananas, Apples, Grapes, Peaches, Pineapple, Pears, Oranges, Berries

VEGETABLES

Green beans, Spinach, Corn (sweet), Broccoli, Turnip or collard greens, Cabbage, Squash, Beets, Rutabagas, Potatoes, Garlic, Vinegar and low-fat salad dressing

Chapter 3

BLOOD SUGAR

I'd like to talk to you about a magical secret that is the key to losing weight, keeping it off and never having it come back. When I decided to change my lifestyle to live fully and feel better, I focused on getting my blood sugar level back within the normal range. I wanted to keep from going on insulin. I wasn't thinking about weight loss. Realizing how blood sugar, weight loss and high energy are connected was the greatest discovery I ever had made.

I lost 80 pounds in eight months, an average of 10 pounds a month. Sometimes I dropped one, two, or three pounds, but always a steady weight loss. And I've kept it off. My health is better than it ever has been in my life, and my energy level is very high.

That's why I emphasize the key to weight loss is carefully monitoring food intake because food intake affects my blood sugar. Your blood sugar is the gasoline on which your body runs. Without a proper blood sugar, your body has a hard time functioning.

I assume since I never have understood the importance of a good blood sugar that many people don't. People with low blood sugar, known as hypoglycemia, have a blood sugar level that is way down on one side. Folks with very high blood sugar, like I had, have diabetes.

The pancreas is the secret to your body's blood sugar since it's the organ that sends out the insulin to regulate your blood sugar. A diabetic is either unable to use insulin

properly, has an insulin deficiency or is not producing insulin at all.

The workings of the pancreas and the numbers of factors affecting it are very interesting. But I want to go over the mechanics of what takes place when you eat and help you understand why being careful about your blood sugar influences whether you gain or lose weight.

BLOOD SUGAR TESTER

The best investment you can make is a little machine to check your blood sugar. Dr. Albritton suggested I check my blood sugar about every two hours throughout the day. Then I could plot the curve of my blood sugar. He wanted me to break the cycle of my blood sugar — stop the lows and level out my blood sugar curve.

Checking your blood sugar levels during the day and night for several days is the only way to learn what's going on with your body. For example, my blood sugar may test 78 at 3:00 p.m. What does that number mean? The normal range of blood sugar is between 60 and 120. Although a 78 reading is OK, my blood sugar is starting to get a little low — especially since I won't eat until after 6:00 p.m. I realize I need to eat some fruit to level out my blood sugar to keep it from going down any more. Then I'll keep a high energy level, and my brain will work sharply without my hitting a tired, late afternoon low.

TRAFFIC REGULATOR

I use a blood sugar testing machine called an Exacto Tech. It has a calculator on it and plastic tabs that slide in a groove to run the test. The kit includes a needle to prick your finger. Although this machine costs about $100, you usually can get a rebate on one when you buy the tabs to use with it.

This machine is very easy to use. I prick my finger to get a drop of blood to put on the center of one of the plastic tabs. I slide the tab in the machine and push the start button. Numbers will start rolling on the calculator. Approximately 30 seconds are required to get a reading.

This test will give me vital information for my well-being. Not having this very important information is like going on a trip without a road map. You don't know where you are. If you go to the doctor, the test at his office may show your blood sugar is fine. It may be at that one time during the day, but probably not all day.

WITHOUT THE PROGRAM

Since blood sugar is the most critical ingredient in being successful on this program, you need to understand your body's blood sugar. Let's go through a typical day and discuss why it goes up and down. Please keep checking the blood sugar chart as we plot the curve.

MORNING — 7:00 A.M. OR WAKE-UP CHECK

When you wake up in the morning, your blood sugar level is called fasting blood. If you're average, your blood sugar will read 70 at 7:00 a.m. Dr. Albritton suggested I take my blood sugar as soon as I wake up each day.

From 7:00 to 9:00 a.m., your blood sugar will make a general rise. It may be a little high at 8:00, or it may not. But let's just say it goes up to 130 at 9:00 a.m. The normal range of blood sugar is between 60 and 120, but it can go up to a 150 and not be out of range. My blood sugar was 330 when the doctor checked me, which is diabetic high blood sugar and very BAD.

9:00 A.M. CHECK

The second time to take your blood sugar is at 9:00 a.m. After you eat the breakfast of a normal, average person, your blood sugar will start a fairly deep decline after 9:00 a.m. (See the chart). Eating breakfast probably sent your blood sugar up to 130, and it now has dropped to 90. Between 90 and 130 is your energy level. If your blood sugar lies between these numbers, you'll have plenty of zip. You're like a band saw. You can go, go, go. But what happens to your blood sugar two hours after you have fried eggs, toast, jelly, a cup of coffee, bagels, doughnuts and all that good garbage?

SUGAR AND CAFFEINE CAUSE BIG DROP

Your body receives the food that comes into it, converts the food into blood sugar and uses energy from the food very quickly, especially sugar products. Suddenly you run out of gas, and you start plunging. Your blood sugar will drop, cross under the 90 mark and perhaps go on down to about 40. This reading is considered hypoglycemic or low blood sugar.

Here's the time of day when everybody gets nervous. As you start crashing at mid-morning, all kinds of bad things start happening. You get headaches, become nervous and grouchy, feel bad and are very fatigued. Make a red circle around this danger point on the chart.

If you eat a usual snack like a cup of coffee, a diet drink, a candy bar, a doughnut, etc. at this low point, suddenly that snack kicks your blood sugar level back up. Then you think you're doing OK and are back up to the good level on the chart. But your blood sugar will drop again quickly before lunch when you eat sugary foods or caffeinated beverages.

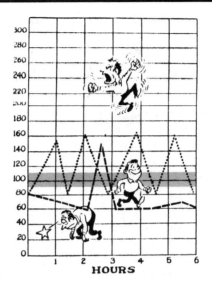

MAN ON TOP OF CHART IS REPRESENTED BY DOTTED LINE. HIS HIGH MARKS INDICATE COFFEE, SWEETS, OR JUNK FOOD INTAKE. HE HAS HEADACHES, IS IRRITABLE AND TIRED AT LOW SPOTS. HIS BLOOD SUGAR IS WAY TOO HIGH. HE'S RIDING A ROLLER COASTER ALL DAY.

THE MAN ON BOTTOM IS REPRESENTED BY BROKEN LINE. HE EATS NO BREAKFAST_ STARTS DAY OFF ON LOW BLOOD SUGAR. COFFEE AND SWEETS PICK HIM UP AROUND 9 A.M. BUT, HE QUICKLY DROPS BACK TO HIS OLD DOG-TIRED, SLEEPY STATE WITH HEADACHES_ AND A BRAIN SO SHORT OF NOURISHMENT THAT IT CAN'T REMEMBER VERY WELL OR FUNCTION AS IT SHOULD.

THIS STIPPLE LINE REPRESENTS A PERSON WHO EATS A GOOD, HEARTY BREAKFAST, AND ABOUT 9:30 A.M. HAS AN APPLE WHICH KEEPS THE BLOOD SUGAR IN THE SAFE ZONE UNTIL LUNCH. THIS PERSON WILL FEEL GOOD WITH PLENTY OF ENERGY TO PERFORM THE JOB AT HAND. AT 3:30 P.M. THEY WILL EAT AN APPLE, BANANA, PEAR, OR SIMILAR FRUIT. THEN, ABOUT 30 MINUTES BEFORE RETIRING, THEY WILL AGAIN HAVE A PIECE OF FRUIT. THIS PERSON'S ENERGY LEVEL WILL RANGE BETWEEN 90 AND 110 ALL DAY. HE OR SHE WILL BE HAPPY ALL DAY AND HAVE A GOOD MENTAL ATTITUDE.

LUNCH

Measure your blood sugar level again at noon. The straight line on the chart is 12:00 noon. Then it shows your blood sugar drops back down, and you're ravishingly hungry. What do you probably do? You eat everything in sight at lunch. Suddenly your blood sugar will rise again — probably as high as it did at 9:00 a.m. Then you're feeling OK again like the chart shows.

3:00 P.M. CHECK

At 2:00 in the afternoon you're still OK, but by 3:00 p.m. you start falling. Take your blood sugar level again. By about 4:00 p.m., you're in trouble again with headaches and nervousness and feeling very stressed. You may drink a cup of coffee to wake you up; however, coffee is the worst thing you can do to your body and your blood sugar. (See Chapter 5 on caffeine).

DINNER

After you eat dinner, you'll cross back over to the good side of your blood sugar for a couple of hours. You start feeling better. Take your blood sugar level around 6:00 or 6:30 p.m.

8:00 P.M. CHECK

Then at 8:00 or 9:00 p.m., your blood sugar will drop again. You'll feel it. Take a blood sugar reading. Most of the time when your sugar gets low again, you'll grab something else to eat to get out of the danger zone. That snack will perk you back up until bedtime.

WHY MOST OVERWEIGHT PEOPLE
HAVE A TREMENDOUS PROBLEM

What your body has experienced all day is a series of highs and lows. You can see on the chart where the trouble spots are circled in red. I'm not going to talk about will power. LOSING WEIGHT AND WILL POWER ARE NOT EVEN SYNONYMOUS. WILL POWER HAS NOTHING TO DO WITH THIS PROGRAM.

Here's what happens. When your blood sugar drops below 70 and especially when it gets into the 60s in mid-morning, your brain will tell your stomach to growl because you're hungry. Actually you're not hungry. You just ate a big breakfast. You're out of blood sugar — gasoline — on which your body can run.

Your body knows the only way to get blood sugar is to eat. At this point we get in trouble. We understand from habit that if we eat a sugar product, our energy level will rise quickly. We'll pick up a sugar product of some kind — cookies, cake, candy bar, anything. Our energy (blood sugar level) will kick up slightly.

But every time your energy level rises with sugar, it drops fast again. That's why folks have to drink coffee all day. Although the caffeine raises your blood sugar level, the more you drink, the worse it is on your pancreas. The sudden highs and lows will finally overwork the pancreas, and it won't know what to do.

The pancreas will start swinging wildly. It either will swing low and you'll have a low blood sugar, or it will swing high like mine and you'll have diabetes. The pancreas is the most important organ in the body to prevent disease. Don't mess with your pancreas.

NO MORE SUGAR AND LESS PROTEIN

Refined sugar and too much protein in your diet will overstimulate and overwork the pancreas. Too much protein in your food intake causes your pancreas to excrete excess pancreatic enzymes. You don't want to waste this important cancer fighting enzyme by eating too much protein.

I learned that to feel good and have my pancreas work at its best, I had to cut down on protein and fats and eliminate sugar. Complex carbohydrates like those found in fresh fruits, vegetables, beans and natural whole grains were best for my body's energy level.

Complex carbohydrates also provide fiber in your diet and contain one-third the calories found in fat and simple carbohydrates like sugar. Complex carbohydrates convert to fat and provide long-term energy. Simple carbohydrates, like sugar, give a short "rush," and then you'll experience a big drop-off of energy. (See Chapters 10 and 11 for more about sugar and fat).

EATING THE PROGRAM WAY

Here's what happened with my breakfast when I ate what Dr. Albritton recommended. You'll see by the red line on the chart how this food program keeps your blood sugar in the safe area of the range.

Your body will get a good start on its day with Old Fashioned Quaker Oats. In the studies I've read, oats generally tend to lower cholesterol.

BREAKFAST

When you eat the program breakfast, your incline line on the chart is virtually the same as any other food, junk food or anything else. Your blood sugar will go up. But oats take three to five hours to digest. When the oats are eaten along with fruit sugars, the oats hold the fruit sugars. The digestion period for releasing the sugar will be slow.

The oats allow the curve to flow in a gradual decline. You will lose that peak you feel after eating a regular breakfast. Your blood sugar may not ever drop below 90 in the morning after this breakfast. Sometimes you will, but sometimes you won't. If you do drop, eat a piece of fruit. You'll be fine.

LUNCH

By lunch time, you'll find you are not ravishingly hungry. What has happened? You have bypassed the cycle that makes you eat.

If you eat the program lunch—baked chicken and three vegetables you can buy or prepare anywhere—you have eaten properly. Your blood sugar will follow the gradual, curved red line on the chart by eating this particular breakfast and lunch and receiving the benefits of these good enzymes. Your afternoon blood sugar levels will not drop as sharply. Also, you won't be ravenously hungry at supper time.

If your energy level dips around 3:30 p.m. or right before bedtime, then eat an apple, peach, pear, orange, handful of grapes, or any fruit you want. You'll experience a slow and gradual curve all day long. Notice on the chart that you never get below the good energy level line.

PUT ZIP BACK IN YOUR LIFE
AND THROW AWAY THOSE ANTACIDS

What does keeping your blood sugar level mean? You'll have much more zip and go power than most people. Today in my early 60s, I have more energy than I've ever had. All kinds of strange things will start happening to you once you eat properly.

For instance, I started this program on a Monday. Tuesday was the last day I had indigestion. Before I began the program, I had kept a roll of antacids in my shirt pocket for 15 years as well as a big box of them on the dashboard of my truck. Every time I ate I'd get indigestion. Now I'm free from indigestion and antacids.

ALL FOOD CALORIES ARE NOT EQUAL

Recent studies show that foods containing equal calories may have different tendencies to raise blood sugar. The foods used in this program Dr. Albritton suggested for me are slow to raise blood sugar, which is good.

This chart, printed in American Health (January-February 1984), shows how various foods raise blood sugar. The serving size of the foods are calculated to have the same number of calories.

The tendency of foods to raise blood sugar is measured by a system referred to as the "glycemic index." It uses glucose as the food to measure up against all other foods, because glucose has the greatest tendency to raise blood sugar.

Fructose, the simple sugar found in many fruits and vegetables, has a relatively low glycemic index and causes a slower rise in blood sugar than the equivalent calories in a potato or cereal. Foods with a low glycemic index raise the blood sugar slowly and include fructose, fruits and complex carbohydrates.

This slow rise allows your body to have a smooth, more level blood sugar, which helps eliminate the highs and lows that make you feel bad. Eating foods with a low glycemic index will keep your blood sugar curve in a smoother line.

How Foods Raise Blood Sugar
(low Glycemic numbers are best)

HONEY AND SUGARS		ROOT VEGETABLES	
Fructose	20	Sweet potatoes	48
Sucrose	59	Yams	51
Honey	87	Beets	64
Glucose	100	White potatoes	70
		Carrots	92
BREAD, PASTA, CORN, RICE		Parsnips	97
Whole wheat spaghetti	42		
White spaghetti	50	PEAS AND BEANS	
Sweet corn	59	Soybeans	15
Brown rice	66	Lentils	29
White bread	69	Kidney beans	29
Wheat bread	72	Black-eyed peas	33
White rice	72	Chickpeas	36
		Lima beans	36
BREAKFAST CEREALS		Baked beans	40
Oatmeal	49	Frozen peas	51
All-Bran	51		
Shredded wheat	67	ODDS AND ENDS	
Cornflakes	80	Peanuts (high in fats)	13
		Sausages	28
FRUITS		Fish sticks	38
Apples	39	Tomato soup	38
Oranges	40	Sponge cake	46
Orange juice	46	Potato chips	51
Bananas	62	Pastry	59
Raisins	64	Mars Bar	68
DAIRY PRODUCTS			
Skim milk	32		
Whole milk	34		
Ice Cream	36		
Yogurt	36		

Chapter 4

EXERCISE YOUR WAY TO GOOD HEALTH

My hope is for you to aim toward a goal of becoming healthy, not just losing weight. You need to plan your week to include exercise as well as to eat nutritionally good food. You can make your body healthier and your immune system strong through what you eat, but ... and this is important ... you also must exercise.

Exercise is the key to keeping your weight off. As you begin dropping weight, start some modest exercise.

Although I always have liked to run, when I was 80 pounds overweight, I was so heavy my knees, ankles and hips would get so banged up when I jogged that I couldn't do it.

At first I started a modest walking program and then slowly increased the difficulty level of my walking. After I dropped about 50 pounds, I began my old jogging program. Tennis, walking, swimming, bowling, skating, bicycling, karate, dancing and/or aerobic exercise are excellent ways to exercise. Consistency is the key. You must commit to a healthy lifestyle.

Before starting an exercise or a diet program, check with your doctor—especially if you are overweight or have not been exercising. If you are a diabetic or have other health problems, you always should keep your doctor informed when you make a change in your lifestyle.

OUR BODIES

OXYGEN

WASTE

THE CLEANING LADY

WHAT EXERCISE DOES FOR YOU

Exercise puts oxygen into your body, which is critical for all your body systems to work right. The oxygen travels through your blood system and oxygenates your whole body — throwing out all the toxins and burning out the wastes.

Exercise has many functions. Immediately you'll have more energy and more resistance to illness and injury, and you'll be able to think clearer. Studies show that exercise can lower blood pressure, reduce levels of artery-clogging blood fats, build up your lungs, reduce the desire to smoke, strengthen muscles and slim down your body shape.

Exercise can reduce stress and keep your mind clear. A good workout can increase your mental energy. However, have a balance, and don't push yourself into exercising beyond your limits. If you turn exercise into a competition with yourself, then you'll just create more stress and lose some of the benefit of that exercise.

Exercise can help you sleep better, which also will reduce stress levels. Regular light exercise in the early

WE **ALL** NEED EXERCISE

evening has been shown to improve sleep. I recommend light walking, jogging or swimming.

BODY METABOLISM — HOW IT WORKS

Exercise is also very important in keeping off your excess weight. Ninety percent of people like me who have kept weight off exercise regularly.

Exercise works by raising the body's metabolism (how your body uses energy). Exercise helps the body to burn fat evenly and helps cut out the highs and lows of blood sugar levels.

Your metabolism is the thermostat on your furnace. When you turn it up, you use more energy. If you turn it down, you use less. But your body's metabolism stays up even when you are resting if you exercise regularly. Your metabolism is burning fat even when you're not exercising.

EXERCISE IS KEY TO THIS PROGRAM

If you don't exercise and go on a low-calorie diet, you may burn up muscle as well as fat, which is unhealthy. A low-calorie diet like I'm on actually can slow down your metabolism. The body is careful about using too much energy in case of famine and starvation. You need to exercise at least 30 minutes a day, three times a week.

But make no mistake, you can't run 80 pounds off. For example, you must eliminate or burn up 3,500 calories to equal the calories in one pound.

Running one solid hour burns up about 800 calories. I'd have to run 4-1/2 hours a day to lose one pound. Let's face reality. I can't run off a pound in a week.

However, exercise tones your muscles, circulates oxygen through your body and speeds up your metabolism. Exercise even may make you more hungry. But don't worry, because if you eat the right kinds of foods, it will give you energy. Then you can go on about your business while feeling good.

WALKING IS GOOD EXERCISE

Jogging may be too strenuous for your joints. Instead, you can walk at least 30 minutes at a time three or four times a week. Walking burns nearly as many calories per mile as jogging and is not as hard on your knees and other joints. Both walking and jogging can be done almost anywhere and at any time without expensive equipment. But be sure to wear the proper shoes for any exercise you do.

Give your muscles a workout. For the best workout, you need to walk fast or play hard enough to feel your heart beating faster for 30 to 45 minutes at a time.

HEART-HEALTHY

Experts suggest that you start walking 20 minutes a day and slowly work up to one hour a day for the best, heart-healthy exercise. Then work on your speed until you can cover four miles in an hour.

BUT EVEN A LITTLE EXERCISE
GOES A LONG WAY

If a vigorous exercise program is not your style, don't worry. You still will benefit from moderate exercise. Besides walking, you can exercise as you go through your day. Take the stairs instead of the elevator. Park at the far end of the parking lot, and walk to shopping or work. Be creative, and keep moving.

OFFICE WORK OR TRUCK DRIVING

If you sit most of the day, you need to break frequently, stretch, take a few deep breaths and walk around for a few minutes — particularly if you drive for a living like long-distance truck drivers. Remember, exercise can make your mind more clear than a cup of coffee can.

HOUSE CHORES AND GARDENING ARE
EXERCISE

You don't have to leave home to exercise. Many studies show that even though running has the advantage of burning more calories faster, gardening and doing house chores burn calories, too, and are good exercise.

Working out as you do your chores has other advantages. You'll have a clean, vacuumed house, a well-cared-for, mowed lawn, or fresh vegetables from your garden.

If you just add a 15-minute walk to your day, you can burn about 100 calories, which is a loss of 700 calories per week or 10 pounds per year.

A good book on exercise is Fitness Without Exercise by Bryant A. Stamford, Ph.D. and Porter Shimer (Warner Communications Company, 1990). The authors redefine fitness and advise a less physically demanding and more overall good health definition. Their concept includes lower cholesterol levels, a diet low in fat and high in fiber and building lean muscle as well as having emotional fitness.

BUILD BACK LEAN MUSCLES -
A STRENGTH PROGRAM

As we age, we lose our shapely, lean, muscle tissue and add body fat — even if our weight stays the same. You must exercise to stop that trend and gain back the lean muscle that has been lost.

A strength program that combines exercise and weights will work best. The American College of Sports Medicine recommends that an efficient, 20-minute strength training workout twice a week will build muscles. The important thing is to seek good instruction.

If you want to lift weights, you will need a qualified instructor to teach you basic safety. Then you won't hurt yourself. Also the instructor can help you get on the best program. A proper weight-lifting program can be learned quickly and can be done safely at home. You don't have to spend a lot of money to build strength.

Just one simple change when you walk can add muscles. As you take your walk, start swinging your arms while holding one-pound weights or one-pound cans of beans to improve the strength of your upper body, your arms and your hands.

IF YOUR GOAL IS TO LOOK GOOD

Of course, if you are like many Americans, your goal in weight loss is to look good in a swimsuit. Then you'll have to do exercises that build muscles or firm specific areas of your body. Participate in an exercise program at your YMCA or local fitness center to reach your goal.

Although these exercises also will improve your overall fitness, keep in mind that they likely will require more effort and time. But anything that makes you feel better about yourself must be good for you, especially if it involves good exercise.

PREVENT DISEASES AND SLOW AGING

Exercise is very important in preventing many kinds of serious diseases. Studies show that lack of physical activity plays an important role in the development of heart disease, the onset of diabetes, high blood pressure or hypertension.

Exercise also can slow the signs of aging. A study performed by Professor Wendy Kohrt at the Washington University Medical School suggests that people should have an active exercise program their entire life. Her study showed that people even up to age 100 benefited from exercise.

Her program included walking, jogging and high-intensity weight lifting. She found people who were 70 got the "same relative benefits as those who were 60." The participants were stronger and felt better. As we age, we will have fewer falls, accidents and breaks if we keep our bodies strong.

PREVENT HEART DISEASE

A study of letter carriers conducted by Dr. Timothy C. Cook of the University of Pittsburgh showed that walking lowers the risk of heart disease. The letter carriers walked an average of five miles a day and had higher levels of the good HDL cholesterol than people who didn't walk.

Good cholesterol works against the bad cholesterol to improve blood circulation. Exercise also helps keep blood pressure normal. Regular aerobic type exercise even may lower at-rest blood pressure.

Vigorous exercise also keeps fat in control, which helps to lower blood pressure. University of Minnesota researchers conducted a study on 900 men and women, ages 45 to 69 with mild high blood pressure (diastolic — lower number — pressure of 90 to 99). The four-year study of those who engaged in moderate exercise of walking, bicycling or calisthenics 2-1/2 hours per week and who ate 25 percent less sodium and limited their alcohol intake showed that 59 percent of the people saw an improvement in their diastolic and systolic pressures.

If you know you have high blood pressure, be sure your doctor evaluates you before you begin an exercise program.

EXERCISE TO AVOID TYPE II DIABETES

Recent studies have shown that exercise may prevent non-insulin dependent type II diabetes in people who have a risk for the disease. Exercise has been utilized

successfully for years to manage those patients who already have this form of diabetes.

Major risk factors for getting diabetes include having diabetes in the family and being obese and of advanced age. More people in certain ethnic groups are affected. If you are Hispanic, Native American or African American, you are at greater risk. If you are at risk, take charge, and work to prevent getting the disease. (See more about diabetes in Chapter 11).

Get off the couch, turn off the TV, and go for a walk or a jog. You'll start enjoying life more, and you'll live a longer, healthier life.

REMEMBER:

o   Exercise helps control weight and keep it off.

o   Exercise turns up your metabolism to burn fat.

o   Exercise puts oxygen in your bloodstream, which gives you energy and gets rid of toxins and waste in your body.

o   Exercise helps maintain an ideal blood pressure.

o   Exercise helps you think better.

o   Exercise can decrease the risk of heart attack, strokes,   diabetes and osteoporosis.

o   Exercise relieves and helps control stress.

o   Exercise makes you feel better and reduces depression.

Chapter 5

CAFFEINE

Coffee is one of the main culprits of blood sugar problems. Personally, I wonder if you ever can lose weight and keep it off if you drink coffee, strong tea and soda pops with caffeine or eat chocolate or any other foods containing caffeine.

Two weeks after I got on the food program Dr. Albritton recommended, I stepped on the scale. I was 10 pounds lighter. Remember, I wasn't even thinking about weight loss. I was focused on my blood sugar—trying to get away from a 330 mg blood sugar level. I didn't want to take insulin the rest of my life. I wanted to get my blood sugar back in the normal range. I found by using this program that monitoring your blood sugar is tied to weight loss. I was delighted when I lost 10 pounds. I thought something I was doing was working! I kept on the same program and didn't change.

A SUDDEN JUMP IN BLOOD SUGAR

As I carefully monitored my blood sugar, my weight just kept falling off, off, off. One morning, my blood sugar had jumped up to 260, which is very high. I had been eating the same breakfast each day as outlined in Chapter 2. I hadn't changed anything. I got worried.

I started taking out one element at a time and checking it each morning. I was thinking maybe the pineapple was a little too rich in sugar or perhaps the culprit was the raisins or the grapes. I checked it for a week but found nothing. The curve on my graph remained smooth and the same

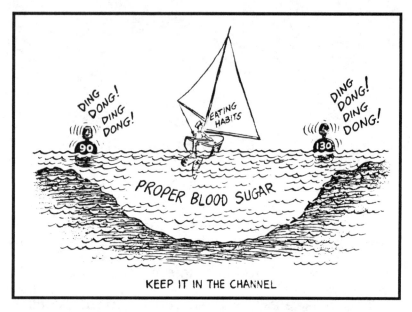

KEEP IT IN THE CHANNEL

as it always did. Then I recalled I had a cup of decaffeinated coffee the day my sugar raced up — not regular coffee — but decaffeinated still has some caffeine in it.

CAFFEINE IS THE CULPRIT

The next morning when I got up I had my regular breakfast and drank a cup of decaffeinated coffee. When I took my blood sugar as usual at 9:00 that morning, boom, it was 260 again. I knew I had the culprit: caffeine!

I've had lots of people tell me, "I can't get up without a cup of coffee, because if I don't drink the coffee, I'll get a headache."

You get a headache when you don't drink coffee because your blood sugar has dropped down to the bottom. You haven't put any gasoline in your tank.

CAFFEINE RAISES BLOOD SUGAR TOO FAST

Caffeine will raise your blood sugar. When caffeine enters your pancreas, it secretes insulin into your body. If you haven't eaten anything, caffeine will pull the glycogen out of your muscles, through the liver and convert what reserve insulin you've got, which is in the form of glycogen. It'll pull the blood sugar into the rest of your body and raise your blood-sugar level.

44

Although you have been feeling bad, you'll start feeling better once your blood sugar rises. When your blood sugar count climbs above 70, your headache will go away. However, the caffeine just keeps your blood sugar going up and up to about 260 before it drops like a rock. Consequently, all of the blood sugar has gone out of your body, and your blood sugar level has crashed below safe levels.

SUGAR AND CAFFEINE, A BAD COMBINATION

Suddenly you are hungry. If you eat something with a large amount of sugar and drink coffee, your blood sugar goes up even higher. Then it will drop like a rock. You're in even more trouble.

YO-YO EFFECT ON BLOOD SUGAR
AND ENERGY LEVEL

So what do you do? You think you've got to have another cup of coffee, more sugar, more sweets and/or more soda products. Consequently, your energy and blood sugar level resembles a yo-yo — up and down, up and down.

If you take a coffee break in the morning or afternoon, remember these two of the five "no's":

NO CAFFEINE — NO SUGAR

Eat a fruit or a vegetable instead of a caffeine drink and a sugar snack. If you can break the caffeine and sugar cycle, you will develop the smooth curve like the one shown on the healthy blood sugar chart. You will bypass your morning crisis and avoid the drops for a smooth curve.

ELIMINATE CAFFEINE AND SUGAR
AND FEEL GREAT

Leave off the caffeine, and you'll keep your blood sugar in the high-energy level. You'll be feeling as wide open as a switchblade knife and going all day long. The headaches will go away, as will the jittery feelings and the fatigue.

CAFFEINE LINKED TO HIP FRACTURES

There are more reasons to leave off caffeine. Studies show that caffeine robs the body of calcium needed for strong bones.

A recent Harvard University study of 84,000 middle-aged women showed that women who drank more than four cups of coffee or colas containing caffeine were about three times more likely to suffer hip fractures than women who drank little or no caffeine. Of course, caffeine also affects men's calcium needs.

AVOID CAFFEINE DURING PREGNANCY

Pregnant women should avoid sodas with caffeine and coffee. This statement is plain common sense since

whatever the mother puts in her body will go into the baby's body also. High caffeine intake has been linked to birth defects, spontaneous abortion and premature births in animal studies.

CAFFEINE INTERFERES WITH
EFFECTS OF MEDICINE

Too, be aware that caffeine may interact with prescription and non-prescription drugs in unpredictable or undesirable ways. If you drink a lot of coffee or sodas, ask your doctor or pharmacist to look at the drugs you take to be sure they are safe with the combination of drugs.

SUGAR AND CAFFEINE DEPLETE VITAMINS

Sugar and caffeine also deplete the vitamin B complex in your body. These vitamins are very important to keep your immune system healthy and to keep your hormones in balance. (See Chapter 7)

Many people drink caffeinated products as a pick-me-up. But, instead of relieving fatigue, caffeine actually can make you feel even more tired and irritable and will disturb your sleep patterns. You may be overstimulated to the point of even greater exhaustion and cause more damage to your immune system. The best way I can explain it is to say caffeine aggravates the body. You must give it up.

KICK THE HABIT AND LOSE WEIGHT

Break the caffeine and the sugar cycle, and you can lose weight and stay healthy. Commit yourself to this program and eat the food and snacks recommended.

Losing weight is not a matter of will power, it's a problem of not giving your body the right fuel. Once you start on this way of eating and stick to it, you will lose weight, have more energy, and feel better.

REMEMBER:

o   Caffeine kicks your blood sugar level up too fast and then makes it drop too low.

o   Caffeine depletes the body of calcium and B vitamins and interferes with your immune system.

o   Caffeine and sugar will make you even more tired and fatigued.

o   Caffeine makes losing weight and keeping it off almost impossible.

Chapter 6

THE IMPORTANCE OF VITAMINS AND MINERALS

Vitamins and minerals are essential for your body to survive. Just because you only need small amounts of them doesn't mean they're not important.

In my opinion and from my experience, I don't think you can get enough vitamins or trace minerals from the usual American diet.

"The average American is deficient in vitamins, minerals and other nutrients because the foods he eats does not supply sufficient quantities of these essential substances," says W. Marshall Ringsdorf, Jr., D.M.D., who conducts a practice in nutritional and lifestyle counseling in Birmingham, Alabama.

Vitamins and minerals are very important for good health. Vitamins and minerals regulate the body's metabolism by:

* converting food into energy and living tissue for normal growth as well as for life itself,
* protecting cells and,
* regulating all the other workings of the body.

VITAMINS FIGHT DISEASES

Today, research is showing what many have believed: vitamins are crucial to helping your body fight off cancer and heart disease and to slowing the aging process. Vitamins support the immune system.

The body can't make vitamins. Vitamins aren't a source of energy — the gasoline for the body — but rather

serve as the catalyst or spark for bringing about many changes and reactions in the tissues.

HOW VITAMINS WORK

Vitamins can act either like the spark in the spark plug that fires a car's engine or the oil in the engine that permits the car to run smoothly. Although food is the gasoline, the car won't start without the proper spark and can't run at all without oil. If a particular vitamin is lacking in your body, a recognized set of symptoms can be identified.

Vitamins work like a team in a cooperative effort. A vitamin or a mineral deficiency requires the balancing of other vitamins and minerals as well as the one in which you are deficient. Just taking the vitamin or mineral by itself may not correct the problem and can be dangerous. Check with your pharmacist or doctor to make certain you are balancing your vitamin and mineral supplements.

RECOMMENDED DIETARY ALLOWANCE

A great deal of study has been done on how vitamins work and what they do in the body. Much more is known today about vitamins than was known even five years ago.

The recommended dosage or intake of vitamins you see on many food and vitamin containers are set by the Food and Nutrition Board of the National Research Council and are called the Recommended Dietary Allowance or RDA.

The RDA standards were designed to help healthy people get all essential nutrients. These minimum requirements are for a healthy body. Some of these requirements are considered way too low by researchers today. These standards are very controversial now.

FOOD AS MEDICINE

Many major diseases in the world have been cured by correcting what a person eats. For instance, people who had scurvy like sailors in the last century cured the problem by eating oranges and lemons full of vitamin C.

One of the most controversial and most studied vitamins is vitamin C. The RDA minimum for vitamin C is set at 45 to 70 milligrams (mg), but researchers working with it say you need to have at least 500 mg units of vitamin C every day. Personally I find taking 1,000 mg of vitamin C a day helps me the most. You just can't get enough in an orange.

SOME VITAMINS MUST COME FROM FOOD

You also need vitamin E for your body to work properly. Eating from a food like wheat germ is the most effective way to obtain vitamin E. The enzymes in the wheat germ aid the vitamin E in properly utilizing the food in your body.

Vitamin E works like a catalyst or a spark. A catalyst is necessary to make two or three things work together. Without the catalyst, having the other nutrients present won't help your body. Getting vitamins in certain kinds of food or with other vitamins and minerals is very important for your body to work at its best.

Vitamin E is the most powerful antioxidant, which means it helps prevent cancer cells from forming. Other powerful antioxidants are vitamin C and beta-carotene, which becomes vitamin A.

I like to supplement my diet with vitamin E tablets. Because vitamin E boosts my immune system, I recommend a supplement of 400 IU (international units) every day.

People with serious heart disease can reduce heart attacks by 75 percent by taking 400 to 800 IU daily, according to a study by Dr. Nigel G. Brown of Northwick Park Hospital in London, England.

Some researchers have found that vitamin E will help dissolve fibrocysts in women's breasts, which can be very painful. The recommended dose is 1,000 IU daily for one month, then drop to 400 IU daily.

Also in early 1998, researchers found that vitamin E played a key role in reducing the incidence of prostrate cancer.

B VITAMINS

An interesting study was done in New York City where researchers studied 100 homeless alcoholics. Researchers found that all participants in the study had low blood sugar and were deficient in vitamin B.

When people drink too much alcohol over and over, they develop what is called the "DT's" (delirium tremens) where they imagine things. The doctors give them a quick shot of vitamin B-12 to bring them out of the DT's. The alcohol they had consumed had burned up their B vitamins. Alcoholics' bodies react by becoming very sick. You must have the B vitamins, plain and simple.

NIGHT VISION PROBLEMS

Some people have trouble with night vision and can't drive at night. Your eyes have a built-in protection — a chemical that acts like a screen that comes over your eyes for protection — to help if you're on a sunny beach or in the snow. If this chemical screen remains on your eyes all the time, you'll have a night vision problem. But if you get vitamins A and D for your vision, suddenly that night vision problem will clear up. You'll be able to see as clearly as you once have.

Vitamin A is present in the beta-carotene in carrots and sweet potatoes. Vitamin A is very important for many enzymes to function. You can get D from sunshine and from fish oils. You've got to have it!

IF ANY ONE OF THESE SECTIONS IS MISSING, WE'RE IN TROUBLE!

As you can see, many scientific studies have found that numbers of diseases can be cured or prevented by the food you eat. For more information, carefully read the next two chapters on vitamins and minerals.

MINERALS ARE IMPORTANT, TOO

The way minerals work in the body is similar to how vitamins work. Minerals:

* act as co-enzymes to aid the body in performing its activities and

* are essential for bodily fluids, the production of bone and blood and to maintain the workings of healthy nerves.

But minerals, like vitamins, are required by your body in small amounts. Even though you must have minerals, you can get most of them by eating a healthy diet like the one I follow.

WHERE DO MINERALS COME FROM?

Minerals are found naturally in the earth. Rocks and stones are made of minerals. As the rocks and stones turn into soil, plants pick them up to nourish their healthy growth. Then humans and other animals eat the plants and thus benefit from the minerals.

Some minerals are needed in larger amounts then others. The ones you need more of are calcium, magnesium, sodium, potassium and phosphorus. The trace minerals your body must have include iron, zinc, copper, manganese, chromium, selenium and iodine. But remember you can overdose on minerals if you take extremely large amounts over a period of time.

Use a balanced mineral supplement like the ones found in multi-vitamins. Balancing is important to help the body use the minerals in the right way and not cancel each other out.

Minerals are absorbed better if they are either taken with food or are in a chelated form. Chelated means that the minerals are attached to a protein molecule to help get them into the bloodstream.

TOO MUCH SALT

Your body requires a small amount of sodium or salt for good health. Sodium helps regulate the amount of fluid in your body, your blood pressure level and muscle contractions and helps with the conduction of nerve impulses.

However, the American diet has too much salt. Salt is poured into fast foods as well as canned and refined foods. Too much sodium intake:

*   causes fluid build-up,
*   can lead to high blood pressure, heart disease and strokes,
*   inhibits the blood from circulating the way it should and keeps it from carrying oxygen and nutrients to the body's cells as efficiently and means greater difficulty in getting rid of waste.

When waste builds up in the body, then you are more susceptible to disease.

Turn off the salt. Season your foods with herbs, spices, and lemon juice. When you eat out, order broiled or baked meat, yeast bread, tossed salad and fresh fruit.

Salt or sodium is present in most everything, including medicine, baking powder and even chewing tobacco. If

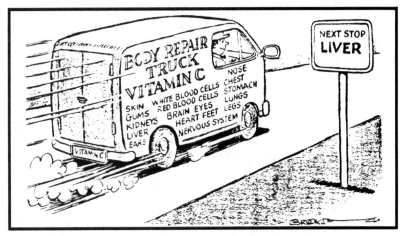

your doctor has put you on a salt-restricted diet, you'll have to watch everything you put into your mouth.

Start studying labels immediately. If one of the first three ingredients is salt, then don't eat the food or use the product. You are the one responsible for lowering your sodium intake.

YOU NEED TO TAKE SUPPLEMENTS

You must have the correct minerals and vitamins in the proper dosages. I highly recommend the fine diet I've shown you. Plus, consider taking the supplements listed here.

You can buy supplements at the grocery or drugstore. The next two chapters will give you more information on vitamins and minerals.

TAKE THESE SUPPLEMENTS DAILY
FOR OPTIMUM HEALTH ·

Multiple vitamins with trace minerals to include zinc and manganese· 1,000 milligrams of vitamin C· B vitamin complex· 400 IU of vitamin E· One cod liver oil tablet

REMEMBER:

o   Vitamins and minerals are essential to life itself.

o   The right food can cure or prevent many diseases, including heart disease, diabetes and cancer.

o   Vitamins and minerals work like a team. You need to keep them balanced.

o   Using little salt is best for your blood pressure, etc.

Chapter 7

BENEFITS AND BEST FOOD SOURCES OF VITAMINS

This chapter is devoted to explaining the benefits of vitamins, the best food sources for vitamins and some of the problems you'll encounter if you are deficient in any of them.

VITAMIN A

I've already mentioned how important Vitamin A is to your vision. Vitamin A also ...

*   is necessary for healthy skin and bone growth,
*   is important for gland secretion,
*   helps your immune system fight infection.

Beta-carotene is turned into vitamin A by the body. Studies have shown that foods high in beta-carotene prevent cancer from developing. The more you eat foods rich in beta carotine, the less likely you are to have cancer of the lungs, stomach, breast, colon, prostate, cervix and/ or mouth. Beta-carotene also may aid your body in curing itself of these cancers, if you already have them.

Without enough vitamin A, your resistance to infection is much lower. Too, you'll have problems with your digestion, dull skin, night blindness and other vision problems.

Good sources for vitamin A are liver, egg yolks, whole milk and butter. Some of the best sources of beta-carotene are green, orange and yellow vegetables and fruits. These vegetables and fruits include cantaloupe, carrots, dried apricots, sweet potatoes, squash, vegetable soup, peaches, papaya, mangos, pumpkin and watermelon. For best protection from illness, eat a combination of some raw and some cooked vegetables and fruits.

B VITAMINS

People often are deficient in B vitamins, which are of ultimate importance in your system. The B vitamins act like a team by working together.

B vitamins help the heart stay healthy and are necessary for good blood circulation. They keep your skin and blood strong and prevent anemia. They also may prevent birth defects.

B vitamins keep your hormones in balance and help your immune system stay healthy. They help you deal with stress and keep you emotionally stable and more alert mentally. When you are under stress, you will need extra B vitamins.

What disease is cured by B vitamins? Some people have such a deficiency in vitamin B that they develop Pellagra and virtually go insane. These vitamins are the ones lacking in the New York alcoholics I mentioned in Chapter 6.

Three tablespoons or one-fourth cup of wheat germ will provide your minimum allowance of B vitamins each day. Other sources are mentioned below. Let's look at the B vitamins one at a time.

THIAMINE — B-1

Thiamine (B-1) is a basic need to keep your nervous system, muscles and heart working at their best. It promotes growth. It is needed for energy production, including the proper use of oxygen and glucose. It helps with your digestion and keeps your mind clear.

A deficiency in thiamine:

* causes loss of appetite and in severe cases, loss of muscle coordination and possible paralysis,

* makes digestion difficult for foods with starches and sugars, resulting in severe diarrhea and extreme loss of weight.

Good sources of thiamine are found in wheat germ, bran and other whole grain cereals. It is also found in pork products, brewer's yeast, green peas and other legumes, beef, kidney, beef liver and sunflower seeds.

RIBOFLAVIN — B-2

Riboflavin (B-2) is an important element in your body to convert protein, fats and carbohydrates into energy. Riboflavin aids your body in carrying oxygen to the body's cells and builds healthy blood, healthy skin, nails and hair, and prevents eye fatigue. Studies show older women need more riboflavin.

A deficiency of riboflavin causes poor growth, fatigue, weakness and dull skin. It also can cause anemia and cataracts. Good sources of riboflavin are almonds, milk, Swiss and Brie cheeses, low-fat yogurt, beef and chicken liver, beef kidney, brewer's yeast and wild rice.

NIACIN

Niacin is a part of the make-up of your body's enzymes that help use protein, fat and carbohydrates. It is important for memory and regulating moods. Lack of niacin can cause dementia or insane behavior—the disease pellagra.

Niacin is essential for healthy skin. It helps to keep cancer from developing. It has been shown to lower blood fats: cholesterol and triglycerides. A deficiency also can cause digestive problems.

Eat grains, wheat germ, almonds, liver, lean meats, poultry, peanuts and peanut butter, dried dates, beef kidney, baked beans and other legumes, sunflower seeds, tuna fish and salmon for niacin.

VITAMIN B-6

Vitamin B-6 or pyridoxine also helps with the immune system and in preventing blood clots. It helps fight against other nervous disorders, too. It's good for healthy skin and helps enzymes work to use fat, protein and carbohydrates. Vitamin B-6 also may protect an unborn baby from some complication.

The lack of B-6 can result in nerve damage and skin problems, especially sores around the eyes and mouth. Too, deficiency of B-6 can mean you'll experience nausea, vomiting and extreme weight loss.

The best sources of B-6 are bananas, whole grain cereals, wheat germ, blackstrap molasses, chicken, fish, potatoes, avocados, egg yolks, sunflower seeds, liver, beef kidney and filbert nuts.

VITAMIN B-12

Vitamin B-12 or cyanocobalamin is essential for all our cells, but especially our nerve cells. B-12 aids your body with memory, concentration, good sleep and balance. It protects the heart from some diseases.

B-12 also helps prevent a serious form of anemia called pernicious anemia. A pregnant woman must get enough B-12 for her baby's health and proper development. People low in B-12 become very irritable. Vitamin B-12 enables our bodies to use fat, protein and carbohydrates.

Good sources of B-12 are milk, Swiss cheese, cheddar cheese, low-fat yogurt, tuna, salmon, eggs, lamb, chicken, meat, liver and kidney. Most of the B-12 we need is synthesized by bacteria that grows in our intestines.

FOLATE — FOLIC ACID

Folate or folic acid is necessary to make RNA and DNA, the genetic materials needed to manufacture and repair all cells. Folate is necessary in producing red blood cells and hemoglobin, which transports oxygen from the lungs to the tissues of the body, and prevents anemia. Folic acid is important to keep your heart healthy and is essential for your central nervous system to work properly.

An estimated 50,000 deaths a year from heart disease in America could be prevented by increasing intake of folic acid, concluded an analysis of 38 studies compiled by Shirley Beresford, an associate professor at the University of Washington School of Public Health in Seattle.

Recent studies at The University of Alabama in Birmingham Hospital have shown folic acid can prevent some cancer of women's reproductive organs. It particularly may help prevent cervical cancer. Pregnant women need to consume plenty of folic acid.

Good sources of folate are leafy greens like cabbage, collard greens, romaine lettuce, wheat germ, bananas, strawberries, cantaloupe, red beets, brewer's yeast, mushrooms, oranges and orange juice, sunflower seeds, some legumes, asparagus, broccoli and lima beans.

PANTOTHENATE

Pantothenate or pantothenic acid, a component of the vitamin B complex, is used to make hemoglobin in the blood and to help the body with some chemical functions.

It is found in many foods, but flour milling and other processing methods destroy it. Good sources are whole grain cereals, most fish and organ meats.

BIOTIN

Biotin helps some of the body's enzymes use food. The best sources of biotin are eggs, milk, turkey and chicken legs, oranges, grapefruit and some berries.

VITAMIN C

Vitamin C has been the subject of many scientific studies, especially in the last 25 years. Vitamin C is a necessary part of the "glue" that holds your body's cells together. It also helps the body use other vitamins.

Vitamin C plays an important role in your body's immune system. The body's first line of defense, lymphocytes in the white blood cells, is absolutely full of vitamin C. Vitamin C can both prevent and fight cancer and heart disease.

A professor of pathology at Oregon Health Sciences University, Benjamin V. Siegel, Ph.D, has studied how vitamin C activates T-cells, the cancer-fighting cells. T-cells are our bodies best defense against cancer. The American Cancer Society recommends you eat foods rich in vitamin C.

Because of vitamin C's ability to boost the immune system, it has been shown to lessen the severity and frequency of colds and the flu. People who have wounds and burns, who have undergone surgery heal faster when their bodies contain high levels of vitamin C. This vitamin also has been shown to activate production of the body's wonder drug: interferon, a protein that inhibits the reproduction of viruses invading the cells and induces resistance to further infection.

Vitamin C also has been found to fight and disable toxic pollutants that we are exposed to daily. This antioxidant activity will keep you young because it slows the symptoms of aging and prevents cancer cells from forming.

A study by UCLA researcher James E. Enstrom showed men getting 300 mg daily may add two years to their lives.

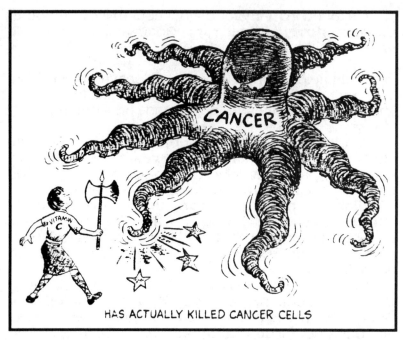

HAS ACTUALLY KILLED CANCER CELLS

A 25-year study by University of Texas researcher Richard Shekelle showed that the men in the study who increased vitamin C intake from 65 mg to 145 mg daily were 28 percent less likely to die of any cause during the study and 49 percent less likely to die of cancer.

Because the stress of an injury or illness lowers the body's vitamin C levels, you need to ingest more of the vitamin when you are sick or injured. Too, vitamin C has been shown to help prevent or at least delay cataracts in the eyes. It helps with rheumatoid arthritis, a connective tissue disease. Vitamin C also improves liver function and helps gums to stay healthy.

Vitamin C helps strengthen the heart and prevent heart disease. It has the ability to cut cholesterol levels and reduces levels of triglycerides and blood fat, both of which promote clogged arteries. Vitamin C also may be an anticlotting agent to prevent heart attack or strokes.

One study showed that women need vitamin C to keep their reproductive organs healthy. Male infertility has been helped by increasing vitamin C intake to one gram (1,000 mg) a day. Vitamin C helps increase sperm count.

Diabetics have a special need for vitamin C since they are susceptible to heart disease, slow healing of bruises and injuries and other immune problems. Vitamin C also reduces insulin requirements. Some diabetics have increased their doses to two grams of vitamin C a day.

If you smoke or drink, you need extra vitamin C. Alcohol causes damage to the liver, and vitamin C can help. In studies, smoking appears to deplete the body's supply vitamin C. Therefore, you must replace that C.

Because of our lifestyles, we require a large daily dose of vitamin C to say healthy and to get well if we become sick or injured. I take 1,000 mg of vitamin C daily. Don't use chewable C, which can harm the enamel in your teeth.

The best sources of vitamin C are fresh fruit like oranges, cantaloupe, grapefruit, lemons, and papaya. Other good sources include fresh strawberries, blackberries, blueberries, tomatoes and juices from grapefruit, oranges, lemons, and tomatoes.

Eat cooked Brussels sprouts, cabbage, cauliflower, baked potatoes, mustard greens and collards and raw or cooked broccoli, onions, garlic, and chives to give your body more vitamin C. Red and green chili peppers and red and green sweet peppers are also high in vitamin C.

Read more about vitamin C in The Vitamin C Connection by Dr. Emanuel Cheraskin, Dr. W. Marshall Ringsdorf, Jr. and Dr. Emily L. Sisley.

VITAMIN D

Vitamin D helps the body use calcium and phosphorus to build strong teeth and bones. Lack of vitamin D can cause a disease called rickets or soft, crooked bones in children. A deficiency in adults can make their bones brittle, fragile and easy to break.

The best sources of vitamin D include milk, cheese, egg yolks, tuna and plenty of sunshine. Vitamin D is absorbed into the body only in the presence of fat.

VITAMIN E

Vitamin E helps your body prevent blood clots. As an antioxidant agent, vitamin E helps keep you young by protecting cells from oxidation, which weakens the cells.

It also helps and protects the immune system and the adrenal and sex hormones. I mentioned other benefits of vitamin E in the previous chapter.

Good sources are vegetable oils, margarine, peanuts and peanut butter, almonds, pecans and sunflower seeds. Vitamin E is a fat-soluble vitamin and must be taken either in oil or with fatty foods.

VITAMIN K

Vitamin K is essential for blood clotting and helps tissue to transfer energy. Milk and vegetable oils are some of the best sources of vitamin K.

Just taking your vitamin pills is not enough for healthy living. You also must eat the right foods and exercise. You don't know how good you can feel until you give this program a try. Believing in yourself is magic.

Chapter 8

MINERALS ARE ESSENTIAL

Minerals are another essential part of our diets. Our bodies can't manufacture minerals. Minerals, like vitamins, are needed in all parts of our bodies: in our brain activity, digestion, reproduction, bone formation and everywhere else.

The minerals we need in larger amounts are calcium, potassium, phosphorus, magnesium and sodium. But we also need small traces of many other minerals including copper, iron, chloride, manganese, sulfur, iodine, zinc, fluorine, chromium, selenium, silicon, vanadium and molybdenum.

Minerals are mostly stored in bone and muscle tissue. You can overdose on minerals, but only if you take an extremely large dose. Minerals can become toxic if these massive amounts are taken for a long time. Let's take a look at some of these important nutrients.

CALCIUM

Calcium is needed for strong, healthy teeth, bones and muscles as well as for the transmission of nerve impulses and to maintain a regular heartbeat. Calcium also is necessary for blood clotting and helps prevent colon cancer.

Several studies, including some by David A. McCarron, Ph.D., of Oregon Health Sciences University, show that calcium can help lower blood pressure.

Extra calcium is especially helpful and necessary if you drink alcohol or caffeine and eat a diet high in salt. These habits deplete the body's calcium and prevent the body from absorbing calcium.

When you don't get enough calcium, you may have these symptoms: aching joints, brittle nails, exzema, heart palpitations, increase in cholesterol levels, insomnia, muscle cramps, nervousness, numbness in arms and/or legs, osteoporosis, rheumatoid arthritis, rickets and/or tooth decay.

Good sources of calcium include whole or skim milk, low- fat yogurt, buttermilk, cheese, almonds, blackstrap molasses, figs, prunes, tofu, oats, broccoli, asparagus, cabbage, kale and collard greens.

To lower blood pressure, McCarron recommends one of these a day: one cup non-fat plain yogurt, one glass of skim milk or three ounces of sardines with bones.

Warning: Soft drinks are high in phosphorus and interfere with the body's ability to use calcium, which may lead to bone loss in adults and poor bone growth in children.

Carefully limit the number of soft drinks you and your children consume, or better yet, just stop drinking them. (See more about the dangers associated with soft drinks in Chapter 5 on caffeine).

COPPER

Copper, a very important trace mineral, is necessary to make bone, collagen (the connective tissue that holds the body together), hemoglobin and red blood cells. It also works to make melanin in your skin, which produces the tan color when you're in the sun.

Copper is very important to your nerves because it aids the production of the myelin sheathing that insulates your nerves. It also helps to regulate cholesterol, metabolism and the heart.

Copper works in a balance with zinc and vitamin C to boost the immune system. Keeping the proper balance of these three is important. If you ingest too much zinc or vitamin C, then your copper levels will drop. Now of course, the opposite also is true. If you take too much copper, then the levels of vitamin C and zinc will drop.

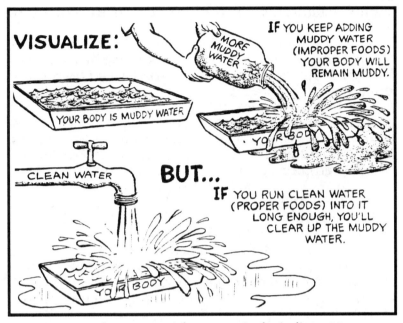

VISUALIZE:

YOUR BODY IS MUDDY WATER

IF YOU KEEP ADDING MUDDY WATER (IMPROPER FOODS) YOUR BODY WILL REMAIN MUDDY.

MORE MUDDY WATER

YOUR BODY

CLEAN WATER

BUT...

IF YOU RUN CLEAN WATER (PROPER FOODS) INTO IT LONG ENOUGH, YOU'LL CLEAR UP THE MUDDY WATER.

YOUR BODY

Most people get enough copper in their diets. However, a sign of copper deficiency is osteoporosis or a weakened spinal column and weakened bones. Also, a degeneration of the central nervous system, a weakness of arterial blood vessels and an enlarged heart may signal a lack of the proper amount of copper.

Red meat, boiled crabs, almonds, avocados, bananas, barley, beans, beet roots, blackstrap molasses, broccoli, dandelion greens, garlic, lentils, liver, mushrooms, nuts, oats, oranges, organ meat, pecans, prunes, radishes, raisins, salmon, seafood, soybeans, and green leafy vegetables are the best sources of copper.

IRON

Iron is necessary for the body to make red blood cells and helps oxygen get into the red blood cells. Iron is required for a healthy immune system and resistance to disease.

Iron also is necessary for your body to use many enzymes and is important for children's growth and energy. Vitamin C improves the body's use of iron by 30 percent.

A lack of iron can cause some of these symptoms: anemia, pale skin, fatigue, dizziness, brittle hair, hair loss and/or nails that are spoon-shaped or have ridges running lengthwise.

Eat raisins, chicken, turkey, liver, molasses, brewer's yeast, almonds, avocados, sweet potato, peaches, pears, yeast, wheat germ, lean hamburger, egg yolks, prunes, pumpkin, lentils, lima beans, soybeans, rice, millet and whole grain cereal to give your body the iron it requires.

MAGNESIUM

Magnesium aids calcium in the formation of strong teeth and bones. It is necessary for enzyme activity and the metabolism of carbohydrates and minerals.

Magnesium also aids in preventing heart disease. Magnesium protects the arterial lining from stress caused by a sudden change in blood pressure. Combined with B vitamins, it also helps reduce and dissolve calcium phosphate stones.

A lack of magnesium can cause nervousness, irritability. dizziness, muscle weakness, twitching and high blood pressure. It helps prevent depression.

Good sources of magnesium include leafy green vegetables, bananas, beans, nuts, oatmeal, peanut butter, whole grains and baked potatoes.

POTASSIUM

Potassium helps prevent strokes and other heart problems. It is needed for a healthy nervous system, a regular heart rhythm, proper blood pressure and proper muscle contraction. It works with sodium to control the water balance in the body. It helps hormone secretion and regulates nutrient transfer to the body's cells.

Stress and the use of diuretics and laxatives can alter your potassium levels. Kidney disorders and diarrhea also can cause problems with your potassium level.

Eat bananas, apricots, avocados, molasses, brewer's yeast, brown rice, dairy foods, fish, meats, poultry, nuts, garlic, dates, figs, raisins, dried fruit, potatoes, squash, yams and wheat bran to get the potassium you need.

CRAWLING THROUGH LIFE ?... WHEN YOU COULD BE SKIPPING THROUGH?

PHOSPHORUS

Most people are not deficient in phosphorus because it is found in most food and, as I mentioned earlier in the calcium section, in sodas. You need to keep a balance of magnesium, calcium and phosphorus because they work together. They will work against each other if there is an excess or insufficient amount of one.

Phosphorus aids the formation of the bones and teeth, the growth of cells and the heart muscle's contractions and is necessary for the kidneys to function correctly. It helps the body to use vitamins and to convert food to energy.

The best sources of phosphorus include asparagus, bran, brewer's yeast, corn, dairy products, eggs, fish, meat, poultry, salmon, dried fruit, pumpkin seeds, garlic, legumes, nuts, sesame and sunflower seeds and whole grains.

ZINC

Zinc boosts the growth and regeneration of the body as well as aids in healing wounds. It sharpens the senses of taste, smell and sight. Zinc also helps the body to keep vitamin E in the right amounts in the blood.

Zinc is a very important mineral because it works with more than 200 enzyme systems affecting almost all body functions. It works in the immune system to zap viral, parasitic and fungal infections.

Many men have been found to be deficient in zinc. It is needed by the prostate gland in men and for the growth of reproductive organs in both men and women. A shortage can cause dry skin, rashes, weight loss, fatigue and mental lethargy. You might notice a numbing of your senses of taste and smell if you lack the proper amount of zinc.

Eat oatmeal, shredded wheat, chicken legs, fish, crab and other seafood, legumes, whole grains, pecans, pumpkin seeds, raw oysters, sunflower seeds, soybeans, mushrooms, lean hamburger and pork chops to get the zinc your body needs.

TAKE WITH FOOD OR IN CHELATED FORM

Chelation means the mineral is attached to a protein molecule that quickly sends the mineral to the bloodstream for absorption. I recommend you buy your supplements in the chelated form. But if you take the mineral supplements with your meal, then they're usually automatically chelated during digestion in the stomach.

Since minerals compete for absorption by the body, you must take minerals in a balanced supplement. Because fiber will reduce the absorption of minerals, take your minerals at a different time of day if you also take fiber supplements.

But remember, taking mineral supplements won't do you much good if you don't eat right. Follow all the diet and supplement recommendations in this book. Then you'll feel great. Good health is an attitude. Get yours right!

Chapter 9

FOOD AS MEDICINE AND MORE

Good health is in your hands. The diseases of this world are like a war against your body. The Good Lord put an army into your body, but to fight disease, that army must have clothes, shoes, equipment and ammunition.

DISARMING YOUR ARMY

However, if you eat fried food, that grease will get in your system and start clogging your blood vessels. If you smoke cigarettes, those heavy metals in the smoke will go through your blood vessels. Cigarettes plaster the grease and the metals down with nicotine tar. Soon the enzymes and oxygen can't pass through the walls of your blood vessels, which often is why smokers are slower to heal.

Then you're disarming your army. When a disease hits, your army should be able to cure that disease. But your body may become overwhelmed with more disease. Your army hasn't got anything to fight since it has been disarmed. Consequently a terrible illness or death may follow.

STAY HEALTHY WITH
A HEALTHY IMMUNE SYSTEM

Your body's army is your immune system, which goes into action whenever your body is being threatened. You can strengthen the immune system and keep it strong by following the good nutrition program I've outlined and supplementing your diet with vitamins.

Antibodies are the soldiers that march in your blood to fight off and kill invading bacteria and viruses. You can boost your body's army. I've found refined sugar messes up my immune system. I'm convinced giving up sugar is very important. (Read Chapter 11 on the problems sugar causes.)

BOOST YOUR IMMUNE SYSTEM WITH VITAMIN C

Although I have discussed vitamin C in depth in the chapter on vitamins, this vitamin is so important I must emphasize it further. Vitamin C helps your body both fight infection and prevent infection.

Taking 500mg to 1,000mg extra vitamin C a day has been shown to prevent or slow down colds. Vitamin C also helps with many other viruses like fever blisters, measles, mumps and pneumonia. Vitamin C also helps fight off bacterial infections like tuberculosis.

PREVENTION AND CURE

What you eat also can help prevent disease. By having a healthy lifestyle, you boost the invisible healers inside of you. By eating a healthy diet and avoiding cancer-causing things like cigarettes, you can reduce the risk of having cancer and diseases.

Studies have found that many viral infections like colds are spread through the eyes by contact with hands. Wash your hands often, especially if you or the people around you are sick.

FIGHT AND PREVENT CANCER

Increase the amount of bulky fiber in your diet, and cut back on fat to help prevent cancer. Fiber makes the digestive track move faster, especially the lower bowel. This action rushes harmful, cancer-causing agents out of the body before they can start causing problems like colon cancer.

ANTIOXIDANTS

Antioxidants help reduce or stop the damage caused by cancer-causing substances. Vitamins C and E, beta carotene, selenium, zinc, copper and manganese are all antioxidants.

The most powerful antioxidant is vitamin E and second most powerful is vitamin C. These antioxidants also help your immune system fight diseases. Beta carotene and vitamin C also can protect you against stroke. (See Chapter 7 on vitamins.)

THE ARMY GOD GAVE US
TO FIGHT OFF DISEASES WITH.

THE SAME ARMY=AFTER
WE'VE DISARMED IT BY EATING
IMPROPER FOODS.

Antioxidants also may help prevent heart disease. A preliminary finding of a recent study at the University of Maryland Medical Center indicates that vitamins C and E can decrease the risk of heart disease caused by a high-fat diet.

Good sources of vitamin C and beta carotene are broccoli, leafy and dark green vegetables, carrots, tomatoes, potatoes and sweet potatoes. The best sources of vitamin E are wheat germ oil and sunflower seeds.

Cauliflower, Brussels sprouts, broccoli, cabbage and other dark and leafy green vegetables fight cancer. All have been found to help fight colon, cervix, rectal and stomach cancers and perhaps prostate and bladder cancer.

D-GLUCARATE REDUCES CANCER RISK

Oranges are high in vitamin C and also contain a high amount of D-glucarate. Oranges help to reduce blood cholesterol and fight plaque in the arteries. Oranges also combat some viruses.

D-glucarate is a potent new discovery in our food. It has been shown to lower cholesterol and to help block cancer in several stages. It is able to suppress excessive cell growth that can lead to cancer. D-glucarate worked both in early and later stages of breast, lung, liver, skin and colon cancer.

Other foods that contain D-glucarate include apples, cherries, bean sprouts, potatoes and broccoli. The body produces some D-glucarate, but researchers say eating foods rich in D-glucaic acid may reduce the risk of cancer.

FOLIC ACID FIGHTS CERVICAL CANCER

Foods rich in the B vitamin, folic acid, have been shown by a study at the University of Alabama at Birmingham to fight cervical cancer in women. UAB's Dr. C. E. Butterworth, Jr., recommends women eat more foods like yellow vegetables and green leafy vegetables, yeast, liver, beans and legumes, citrus fruits and juices. Spinach and broccoli eaten raw are also good. Folic acid is also shown to reduce depression.

OTHER CANCER FIGHTERS

High-fiber wheat bran and wheat germ inhibit breast and colon cancer. You need to eat one-fourth of a cup of bran cereal or wheat germ a day for maximum protection. Radishes are believed to be cancer fighters, too.

RESPIRATORY HELP

Chili peppers help cure problems with your lungs, sinuses, and respiratory system. A substance called capsicum thins the mucus in the lungs. But don't eat too many peppers because they can irritate ulcers and hemorrhoids.

DRINK WATER

Your body needs at least six to eight eight-ounce glasses of water a day. Water is absolutely necessary for life. Our bodies are about 70 percent water. We will die if we lose 20 percent of our body's water.

Water is how food nutrients, oxygen, chemicals like hormones and enzymes, vitamins and minerals are transported in the body. Our bones are even made of 30 percent water.

Plenty of water makes your body perform its functions better. Your blood circulates better, your digestion works better, and you think more clearly. Too, water keeps the muscles toned.

Water is needed to rid the body of waste products and toxins. It helps the kidneys clean the poisons out of the body. About a quart of water flows through your kidneys every minute. If your urine is a dark color or has a strong odor, you need to drink more water.

74

If your body holds water (fluid retention), you need to drink plenty of water to cure it. Drinking more water is much better for your body than taking diuretics because you can grow dependant on diuretics. More water causes the kidneys to make more urine, and more urine means less fluid retention.

BATH

A warm or hot bath can relax you and stimulate your metabolism. Try a warm bath if you can't get to sleep. Everyone knows a bath on a hot day is the best way to cool off. A hot bath soothes muscles and arthritis pain and reduces stress. Follow the hot bath with a cool shower. Don't use very hot water if you have heart disease, high blood pressure or diabetes.

TOO MUCH FAT

Fat is what makes people fat. Fat has more calories than any other source. Reduce your fat to less than 20 percent of your calories. You must have a certain amount of essential fatty acids, about one-third from your food, to live. But your body makes any extra fat it may need from the proteins and carbohydrates you don't use.

That pat of butter on your biscuit, the fat in red meat, the fat you fry with, and fast-food hamburgers are what put on extra pounds. Foods in a high-fat diet also are slow to digest, make you feel sluggish, slow your ability to concentrate and raise your blood cholesterol.

A healthy, balanced diet uses good fats containing essential fatty acids to help the body use food and to produce maximum energy. (See Chapter 10 to find out about how a healthy body needs a combination of good fat and protein).

EAT MORE COMPLEX CARBOHYDRATES

Aim to ingest about 60 percent of your calories in complex carbohydrates. Complex carbohydrates are found in fresh fruits, vegetables, beans and natural whole grains. Complex carbohydrates provide a constant flow of energy.

Carbohydrates like fruit sugar or starches like potatoes are mostly burned up as energy soon after eating and not stored. Complex carbohydrates also contain vitamins and minerals and have fewer calories than fats or refined sugar. Refined sugar is a simple carbohydrate that gives a short-lived rush or turns into stored fat. (See Chapter 11 to learn more about sugar).

FAT IS NECESSARY FOR LIFE

A little unsaturated fat is necessary for your body to work properly. It is saved by the body and burned sparingly to stimulate the metabolism. Two fatty acids, linolenic acid and linoleic acid, are essential for life, but most of our diets are deficient in them. The best oils come from flax and pumpkin seeds, soybeans, walnuts and cold-water fish. (See Chapter 10 on fats).

Fats are digested more slowly than other nutrients and keep you from getting hungry. By speeding up the metabolic rate, the essential fatty acids help to burn off excess fat. To be thinner and stay thin, eat complex carbohydrates and good fat.

FAT RAISES RISK OF CANCER AND HEART DISEASE

Most of us eat too much of the wrong kind of fat, which puts us at a high risk for cancer and heart disease. If you change to a diet low in saturated fats like the program I've outlined, you will cut the risk of heart disease and reduce

the risk of colon, breast and uterine cancer. With a low saturated fat diet, you even may be able to reverse heart disease. (See Chapter 14 on healthy heart).

BREAK THE FAT HABIT

Why do we eat so much fat? If you eat a diet high in red meat, you will ingest a lot of fat. That's why I suggest eating no red meat. Processed meat like hot dogs, Spam, some sandwich meat and sausage also contain a large amount of fat and should not be eaten at all.

Many of us, especially Southerners, have been brought up eating foods flavored with fat. Cooking a pot of greens usually includes adding bacon or ham to the greens or a pat of butter to flavor potatoes and biscuits.

OTHER WAYS TO FLAVOR FOOD

How can you flavor without fat? Many wonderful-tasting spices such as pepper, basil, parsley, thyme, and oregano will enhance the flavors of your foods without adding fat. Fresh or powdered onions and garlic as well as fresh peppers and mushrooms will add flavor. A sprinkle of lemon and dill is delicious on broiled or grilled fish.

Bouillon, vinegar, mustard or lemon juice add fat-free flavors to all kinds of vegetables. There's a wide variety of vinegar flavors from which to choose.

CUT FAT OUT OF RECIPES

Use one-half the amount of fat called for in your favorite recipes. You can substitute plain, low-fat yogurt or applesauce for the same amount of fat in many recipes. Instead of meat in a casserole, use squash, broccoli, red peppers, onions, carrots on whole wheat pasta. Instead of frying foods, cook food in a little water and use only a small amount fat, like a cooking spray.

TAKE OFF THE SKIN

Also cut the fat content in dishes by pulling off chicken and turkey skin before you cook these meats. When you eat meat, cut off all the fat you can. However, the meat itself still will contain fat that may raise cholesterol levels.

Cook meat on a raised broiler pan to allow the fat to drip away. Don't fry anything anymore! Bake, stew, broil, grill or poach everything you eat.

FAT-FREE EATING OUT

When you eat out, order the lean meals. Ask that the fat or skin be removed. Many restaurants and even fast-food places have low-fat or lean items on the menu now. Drink low-fat milk, and eat low-fat cheese, yogurt and sour cream.

Eat fish. Fish is low in fat, and fish oils contain omega-3 fatty acids. Omega-3 are special fats that can keep your heart healthy by lowering the level of the harmful LDL cholesterol in the blood. Fish are also high in vitamins A and D. (See more on cholesterol in Chapters 10 and 14.)

READ LABELS FOR INGREDIENTS

When you shop, check the ingredients in prepared foods like frozen dinners. If the top three ingredients on the label are oil, butter or sugar, don't buy it. Buy canned tuna fish packed in water, not oil. Use low-calorie salad dressing containing reduced-calorie oil.

Since fatty products have more calories than any other food source, to keep your weight under control, reduce your fat to less than 20 percent of your calories. If you cut out one tablespoon of fat per day, you can lose 10 pounds in a year. Simple changes make a big difference.

FAT ZAPPERS

The vegetables listed here have high concentrations of fat-melting ingredients. They stimulate the process of metabolism, which speeds up washing the body cells. This action also accelerates the burning and removal of accumulated fatty deposits from the cells.

The best fat zappers are: dark green lettuce, romaine lettuce, Brussels sprouts, tomatoes, beets, cabbage, carrots, celery, cucumber, endive, asparagus, radishes, garlic and onions. Soybeans contain lecithin, which may be a barrier to fat and reduces its accumulation. Sauerkraut without salt and horseradish are also fat zappers.

Apple cider vinegar or lemon juice taken either by the tablespoon in a glass of water or in salad dressing also works to zap fat. Apples, berries and most fresh fruit high in pectins are fat zappers. They work best if they are chopped finely as in applesauce.

ADD MORE FOOD FIBER TO YOUR DIET

Along with eating too much bad fat, most of us don't eat enough fiber. Fiber in foods fights fat build-up in cells. Fiber is the bulky part of food that is not digested.

BEST FIBER AND NUTRITIONAL VEGETABLES

The most nutrition-packed vegetables were recommended by a consumer group because they contained the most fiber and met the daily requirement of six nutrients.

In order, starting with the best, were the sweet potato without skin, raw carrots, cooked carrots, cooked spinach and cooked collard greens.

You also get a large amount of fiber in fruits, berries with seeds, dried beans, potatoes, brown rice, wheat and oat bran and other whole grains.

FIBER LOWERS CHOLESTEROL,
STOPS CONSTIPATION

Fiber helps your body's digestion by causing the food to move through the body faster. Increasing the amount of fiber in your diet cures constipation. The fiber in vegetables and fruits also has been shown to lower cholesterol.

High-fiber foods are low in calories. That's why you should eat plenty of fruit and vegetables in this program.

Studies have shown that a high-fiber diet can help control diabetes by slowing the body's passing of glucose into the bloodstream from the digestive tract. Fiber also can help diabetics lower their blood pressure.

BOOKS TO READ

I hope this chapter has interested you in learning more about food as medicine. I have more information in the chapters on the "Healthy Heart" and "Diabetes." Here are some books with wonderful information in them. I know you'll enjoy reading them.

Prescription For Nutritional Healing by James F. Balch, M.D. and Phyllis A. Balch, C.N.C. (Avery Publishing Group, Inc., N.Y., 1990).

The Food Pharmacy by Jean Carper (Bantam Books, 1988).

Everyday Health Tips by "Prevention Magazine" (Health Books, 1988).

Health and Happiness by Emanuel Cheraskin, M.D., D.M.D. (Bio- Communications Press, Kansas, 1989).

The Vitamin C Connection by Dr. Emanuel Cheraskin, Dr. W. Marshall Ringsdorf, Jr., and Dr. Emily L. Sisley (Harper & Row, N.Y., 1983).

REMEMBER

o   Your health is your responsibility.

o   You can cut your cancer risk by quitting smoking.

o   You should eliminate bad fat and eat unsaturated fats high in essential fatty acids.

o   You must add fiber to your diet.

o   You can eat fat-zapping food to help you slim down.

o   You need to quit smoking and drink alcohol moderately.

o   You can build your immune system with vitamins C and E and beta carotene.

o   You can improve your health by eating oranges and food high in folic acid.

o   You must drink plenty of water every day.

Chapter 10

FAT, A CLOSE LOOK

Many books have come out since the 1988 report from then-Surgeon C. Everett General Koop on the danger of fats in the diet. But the information I give you is will blow your mind.

First of all, our bodies need fat to survive. Research as early as the beginning of the 1800s shows that the body needs good oil and good protein in combination. Too much protein causes diseases and constipation.

GOOD FAT

Certain unsaturated fats are good for us, but most diets are deficient in them. There are only two essential fatty acids (EFAs), and they are absolutely essential for life, not to mention good health. They cannot be made by the body, so they must come from the food you eat. One is linolenic acid (LNA). The other is linoleic acid (LA), which is considered by many nutritionists to be the most essential fatty acid. The body makes other important substances from it.

But the diets of many Americans are deficient in these nutrients. Udo Erasmus, author of Fats and Oils, estimates that most Americans get only one-fifth of the essential fatty acids they need for good health. Essential fatty acids must come from foods, but they are sensitive to destruction by light, oxygen and high temperatures. They must be stored in dark, airtight containers. Or even better, eaten fresh, which means either eaten raw or ground and eaten within 15 minutes.

These essential fatty acids help regulate your body thermostat and calorie-loss mechanism. So they actually help burn off fats and keep you slim.

FATTY DEGENERATIVE DISEASE

Essential fatty acids are extremely important to the body's health. They are required to make the main structural components of cell membranes called phosphatides.

A 1984 study conducted in Great Britain concluded that a deficiency in EFAs can play a role in arteriosclerosis, coronary thrombosis, multiple sclerosis, diabetes, high blood pressure, and cancer. Large-scale epidemic proportions of these degenerative diseases began only in the past 100 years. One reason is that our modern, highly refined foods don't contain many essential fatty acids because they spoil easily.

Vegetarians and people who eat a diet high in complex, unrefined carbohydrates and/or fish or wild animal meat (which has a low saturated fat content) are not likely to develop fatty degenerative diseases. Dr. Samuel Rosen studied the Mabaan tribe of Africa, whose diet mainly consists of fruits, vegetables and nuts — little saturated fat — and found no high blood pressure, artery clogging or dietary deficiencies. And Greenland Eskimos, Japanese fishermen and Indians of the Pacific Northwest all consume large amounts of fish but rarely develop heart disease.

In countries where only 15 to 20 percent of the diet is fat, there is a much lower problem with fatty degenerative diseases than in countries that eat high-fat diets. So even eating 30 percent of calories as fat is too much. Thirty percent of calories as fat is recommended by the U.S. National Academy of Sciences, the Senate Select Committee on Health and Nutrition, the American Heart Association and the National Research Council.

Contributing causes for susceptibility to these fatty degenerative diseases are the amounts of alcohol, cigarettes, and sunshine (which can destroy unsaturated fatty acids in the body) you are exposed to as well as what types of medications you take, and vitamin, mineral and

CONTINUOUSLY GOVERNS BODY NEEDS
AS WELL AS EVERY LIFE PROCESS

other nutritional deficiencies. How you handle stress, how much you exercise and your attitude toward life all affect your susceptibility to diseases.

HOW FATS WORK

Good fats are digested more slowly and prevent hunger from recurring for up to five or eight hours after eating. Proteins and carbohydrates are digested in two to five hours, and refined sugars in less than an hour, which means hunger recurs sooner, often causing overeating. Essential fatty acids increase metabolic rate and help burn excess saturated fat. So contrary to popular diet advice, not all fats are fattening.

A diet high in refined foods, which are low in essential nutrients, leads to overeating, and this overload of calories can make us fat.

OIL AND PROTEIN

Taking oil or fat totally out of your diet can cause disease. There is a greater sensitivity to toxins if oil and

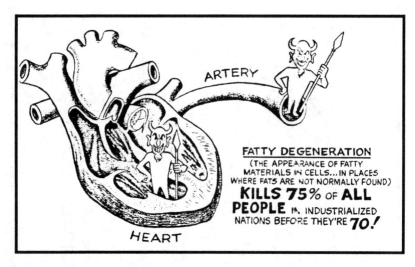

ARTERY

FATTY DEGENERATION
(THE APPEARANCE OF FATTY
MATERIALS IN CELLS...IN PLACES
WHERE FATS ARE NOT NORMALLY FOUND)
KILLS 75% OF **ALL PEOPLE** IN INDUSTRIALIZED NATIONS BEFORE THEY'RE **70!**

HEART

protein are not invested in the right proportions. Sulphur-rich proteins and essential fatty acids work together. Dr. Johanna Budwig, a German scientist, found that linoleic acid reacts with sulphur-containing proteins to form a new product with new properties. The new product attracts oxygen, which is important to all life functions.

GOOD FATS AND THEIR SOURCES

As I wrote earlier, both linoleic acid (LA) and linolenic acid (LNA) are required by the body but must be obtained from food. At least one-third of out total fat intake should be essential fatty acids. Everything alive contains some fats and oils. All living things are made of cells containing phosphatides, which contain fatty acids.

SEEDS AND NUTS

The best source of essential fatty acids are the oils of certain seeds and nuts. Flaxseed oil, also called linseed oil, is best. Hemp seeds, pumpkin seeds, soybeans and walnuts contain both essential fatty acids. The seeds and oils should be stored in dark or opaque containers away from light, oxygen and heat. To get the most nutrition, you should be eat them fresh (raw or ground) and within 15 minutes.

But the oils are difficult to find fresh. To be effective, these oils must be pressed and packaged in the dark without being refined, filtered or deodorized.

GET A SMALL INEXPENSIVE COFFEE OR SPICE GRINDER.
MIX ONE TEASPOON OF FLAX SEED WITH ONE TEASPOON
OLD FASHION QUAKER OATS. THE OATS WILL COVER
THE STICKY FLAX SEED MAKING IT EASIER TO GRIND.

THEN GRIND AND PUT OVER YOUR REGULAR BREAKFAST.
FLAX SEED CAN BE BOUGHT AT HEALTH FOOD STORES OR
AT ANY FEED STORE.

The oils listed below don't contain LNA, but do supply a lot of LA, which is needed even more by the body. This list is in order beginning with the best: soybean, walnut, evening primrose, safflower, sunflower, grape, corn, wheat germ, sesame, rice bran, cotton, canola (rape seed), peanut, almond, olive, coconut palm kernel, beech, Brazil, pecan, pistachio, hickory, filbert, macadamia and cashew.

If you can't get fresh oil, eat the seeds. This is a good way to get the oils, along with the seed's vitamins, minerals, protein and fiber. You need to drink plenty of water when you eat flaxseed because flax swells up to three times its dry volume by soaking up water.

GRAINS

Whole grains contain good quality oil. They are about half LA, but the oils spoil rapidly when the grains are broken, pressed or ground into flour. Refined flours remove all these oils to extend shelf life.

VEGETABLES

Dark green vegetables like spinach, parsley, and broccoli contain small amounts of EFAs. Eat them fresh or right after cooking to avoid the loss of nutrition through oxidation. Fruits are similar to vegetables in fat content.

FISH

Cold water fish like salmon, mackerel, rainbow trout, sardines, and eels contain large quantities of LNA. Seaweed and shellfish supply both essential fatty acids in smaller quantities.

WILD MEAT

Meat from wild animals has a much higher amount of essential fatty acids than domestic animals and also is lower in saturated fat.

POULTRY

Fowl fat contains up to 25 percent LA, which helps to metabolize saturated fats. Commercial eggs are low in LA and LNA.

ORGAN MEATS

Organ meats such as liver are lower in fat and have more EFAs than muscle meats.

DAIRY PRODUCTS

Dairy products contain very few essential fatty acids. Udo Erasmus, a nutritionist, calls butter a "neutral fat," neither good nor bad. But it is not necessary and is dangerous in excess.

RAW FOOD

The more food we consume in its natural raw state, the higher the vitamin content of our diet. Raw foods contain living enzymes that are destroyed through cooking, resulting in more work for our digestive systems.

BAD FATS

Advertisements lead us to believe that polyunsaturated means essential, healthy fat. It doesn't. There are only two essential fatty acids and eight other natural and valuable polyunsaturates, which the body can make from LA or LNA, or can get from foods. But there are hundreds of polyunsaturates possible, many unnatural and some harmful. They don't function like EFAs, and some even interfere with the functions of EFAs.

All oils should be stored in opaque or dark containers away from light, oxygen and heat. Most oil found in grocery stores are in clear containers and are not protected from heat. So they already have lost most of the nutrition that might have survived refinement.

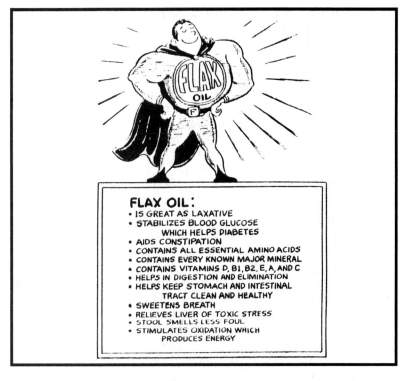

FLAX OIL:
- IS GREAT AS LAXATIVE
- STABILIZES BLOOD GLUCOSE
    WHICH HELPS DIABETES
- AIDS CONSTIPATION
- CONTAINS ALL ESSENTIAL AMINO ACIDS
- CONTAINS EVERY KNOWN MAJOR MINERAL
- CONTAINS VITAMINS D, B1, B2, E, A, AND C
- HELPS IN DIGESTION AND ELIMINATION
- HELPS KEEP STOMACH AND INTESTINAL
    TRACT CLEAN AND HEALTHY
- SWEETENS BREATH
- RELIEVES LIVER OF TOXIC STRESS
- STOOL SMELLS LESS FOUL
- STIMULATES OXIDATION WHICH
    PRODUCES ENERGY

MARGARINE

Avoid hydrogenated oil products. High temperatures, full or partial hydrogenation, deodorizing and other commercial methods destroy EFAs, making them unusable by the body.

ALTERED FAT

Altered fat substances like shortening and margarine don't fit into the precise molecular architecture of our bodies. They take part in uncontrolled free radical chain reactions within the body, resulting in toxic metabolic by-products. Other sources of altered fat include refined oils, baked products, candy, french fries and deep-fried foods and processed convenience foods like potato chips.

PROCESSED FOOD

Most of the fats in sausage meats are saturated. Some of these products also contain starch as fillers, which are converted to saturated fat in the body.

Hundreds of products contain hidden fats, sugars, starches, flavorings, preservatives, and other additives not found in nature. Erasmus calls these substances "an unwelcome addition to the human diet, from the standpoint of health."

THEORIES OF DEGENERATIVE DISEASES
CHOLESTEROL

A diet high in non-essential fatty acids and refined carbohydrates causes an increased cholesterol production by the body. This is why people in the "processed foods" countries have high cholesterol levels.

But a diet that contains the proper amount of essential fatty acids can lower cholesterol levels. Research from several Japanese universities showed that evening primrose oil and safflower oil decreased levels of LDL, the "bad cholesterol," in patients with high levels of cholesterol.

Some types of dietary fiber also help lower cholesterol levels, including fruits, green, leafy vegetables, root vegetables, whole grain cereals and breads.

TRIGLYCERIDES

Triglycerides are the most common form of dietary and body fat. They carry the fatty acids from food or those made in the liver through the bloodstream.

The level of triglycerides in the blood is related to the amount of refined sugars, starches and fats that we eat. The increased use of these refined foods in our diet parallels the increase in cardiovascular disease and other degenerative diseases in the 1900s.

Refined sugars increase the level of triglycerides in the blood. The body transforms refined sugar and starches into the saturated, hard, sticky fats that the body doesn't need. These fats also interfere with the functions of the EFAs in the body.

Some fish, especially cold water fish, contain highly unsaturated fats that lower blood triglycerides and cholesterol and protect against fatty degeneration of inner organs.

DEFICIENCY THEORY

This theory suggests that the cause of degenerative disease is the deficiency of vitamins, minerals, fiber, and

EFAs, which are needed to metabolize cholesterol and fats. Refined sugars, starches and oils all are deficient in minerals and vitamins.

DISEASES OF DEFICIENCY OF FATTY ACIDS

Research on cancer patients by Dr. Budwig as early as 1953 suggested that their blood was deficient in EFAs, phosphatides and albumin, a blood protein. The deficiency stopped when the patients were given 3 tablespoons of flaxseed oil and 4 ounces of non-fat cottage cheese (which contains sulphur-rich amino acids) daily for three months. Budwig used no surgery, drugs or radiation in her treatment.

Along with the fresh flaxseed oil, the patients' diet included carrots, fresh greens, whole grains, skim milk, protein, nuts and a few herbs such as stinging nettles and celeiac for their diuretic effects.

Budwig reported amazing results! Within three months she said the patients' tumors receded and disappeared, anemia was alleviated, energy increased and vitality returned. The symptoms of cancer, diabetes or liver disease disappeared.

REMEMBER

o   Essential fatty acids are necessary for life.

o   The EFAs stimulate metabolism and help burn off excess fats to keep you slim.

o   Eat good fats high in EFAs like flaxseed oil, pumpkin seeds, soybeans and walnuts.

o   Good fats satisfy hunger three times as long as carbohydrates and protein so you won't overeat.

o   Eat more raw vegetables, fruits, seeds and nuts.

o   Avoid hydrogenated oil products like margarine, refined oil, and shortening. They don't fit your body's needs and can interfere with the use of EFAs by the body.

o   Many degenerative diseases are caused by eating too much fat, so limit fat to 20 percent or less of your daily calories.

Chapter 11

SUGAR, AN "ANTINUTRIENT"

Here's more information that will change your view of what you eat forever. Sugar contains nothing but empty calories, yet it is an ingredient in almost all processed foods. But you can lead a healthy, sugar-free life and get back to the true and delicious taste of food.

A SHORT, SHADY HISTORY

Refined sugar is really a newcomer to the diet of man. It has been available in large amounts and at a cheap cost for only the past 300 years. It has a shady history.

By the early 1500s, sugar was becoming an economic force in the world. The control and taxation of sugar created great wealth. After Columbus discovered the New World, sugar soon was introduced, along with slavery, to the European countries. Before long, wars were being fought to control sugar.

In the past 200 years, refined sugar has become a staple of the diets in developed countries. Some nutrition experts blame advertising for what they call "sugar addiction."

In 1990, the American Academy of Pediatrics asked for a ban on food commercials aimed at children, because most of the food was high in sugar. The academy said these sugary cereals, candies and cookies caused high cholesterol and obesity.

ANTINUTRIENT

A U.S. Senate committee found the perfect name for refined sugar when it called it an "antinutrient" in 1973.

In sugar cane or sugar beets, 90 percent of the nutrients are removed to make refined sugar. So instead of adding minerals, vitamins and fiber to your diet, sugar adds nothing but calories.

Sugar also has a negative effect on other nutrients in the diet or stored in the body. The body must use its own nutrients to metabolize sugar. Studies have shown that sugar depletes stores of chromium, magnesium, potassium and thiamine.

CHROMIUM

A deficiency of chromium, a trace element, impairs glucose metabolism. In the past decade, research has suggested a relationship between chromium deficiency and diabetes. Sources of chromium include fresh fruits and vegetables, whole grains, dried peas and beans, and peanut.

MAGNESIUM

Depletions of magnesium, a mineral, may lead to altered heart and mental functions. Sources include whole grain cereals, leafy green vegetables, nuts and soybeans. Be careful, however, when taking magnesium supplements not to take more than the recommended daily allowance of 300 to 400 milligrams, or you may experience fatigue, nausea, vomiting, coma and even death.

POTASSIUM

A shortage of potassium, an electrolyte, causes muscle cramps and other neuromuscular ailments. A deficiency in potassium impairs fluid balance and cellular function. Often people who take diuretics ("water pills") have a problem with potassium deficiency, which can lead to heart irregularities and death. Sources include fresh vegetables and fruit (especially oranges and bananas), peanut butter, dried peas and beans, potatoes, yogurt and meat.

THIAMINE

A deficiency in the vitamin thiamine causes beriberi, a disease that results in weakness, fatigue, loss of appetite, apathy, depression, constipation and memory loss. This deficiency also impairs the function of the heart, nerves

THE MAJOR ADDICTION PROBLEM

and brain. Alcoholics are susceptible to thiamine deficiency because of a poor diet coupled with decreased ability to absorb the vitamin. Sources of thiamine include green vegetables, cereals, beans, milk, pork and beef.

NEGATIVE EFFECTS OF SUGAR

If you eat a diet high in sugar and other highly refined foods, chances are you aren't eating enough nutrient-rich foods. Think about it: If you skip breakfast, snack on sugary junk foods and drink a lot of soft drinks throughout the day, you're not leaving much room for healthy foods.

And that's just the sugar you know you're eating! Sugar is a hidden ingredient in many processed foods. Next time you go to the grocery store, take the time to read the list of ingredients on the foods you buy. You'll be surprised to find sugar in frozen vegetables, soups, salad dressings, cheese, salt substitutes, milk, baby formula, instant coffee and tea, and even sauerkraut!

Children, in particular, are in danger of poor nutrition from a high-sugar diet. In his 1973 study of sugar, <u>Sweet & Dangerous</u>, British researcher Dr. John Yudkin estimated that some children get 50 percent of their calories from sugar. In 1978, the Bogalusa Heart Study confirmed those suspicions, finding 10-year-olds who received 48 percent of their calories from refined sugar.

THE QUICK LETDOWN

Sugar triggers the release of insulin by the pancreas. Insulin metabolizes sugar quickly, but a lot of insulin is left in the bloodstream with nothing left to process. That's why sugar gives you a quick pickup but lets you down ever faster. (See Chapter 3 on blood sugar.)

DIGESTION

Some sources say sugar even can upset your stomach! This theory suggests that when sugar is eaten with other foods, acid fermentation occurs in the warmth and moisture of your stomach. The fermentation of sugar and starches forms carbon dioxide, acetic acid, alcohol and water. Except for water, none of these is needed by the body.

CONTROVERSY

We know sugar can cause tooth decay. The cavity process starts when bacteria mix with carbohydrates — sugars and starches — to make acids. Acids can eat away tooth enamel, causing decay. This cavity-producing action continues every time you eat sugars or starches.

Beyond that, many doctors and nutritionists say that a diet high in sugar is indicated in diabetes, high blood pressure, atherosclerosis, obesity, alcoholism, behavioral disorders and even cancer. The long-term effects of sugar-loading don't look good with the evidence presented so far, but not enough research has been done for scientists to know exactly what role sugar plays in the development of these degenerative diseases.

Other experts say sugar gets a bad rap. They say refined sugar is not a poison and that in moderation as part of a balanced diet, sugar doesn't cause problems for healthy people. But any health expert will tell you that the

more you avoid sugar (and other highly refined foods) in favor of nutritious foods, the better you'll feel.

Sugar substitutes such as saccharin and aspartame do not promote good health any more than sugar does. Once you get accustomed to the natural flavors of food, you'll find sugar and artificial sweeteners taste sickeningly sweet. And you'll be right.

REMEMBER

o   Sugar is a major factor in tooth decay.

o   Refined sugar has no nutrients except calories.

o   Sugar robs the body of nutrients.

o   To find out how good you can feel, eliminate sugar and other highly refined foods from your diet.

o   Eat whole natural grains, fresh vegetables and fruit in season to be healthy.

o   You can control what you eat and be healthy.

Chapter 12

A HEALTHY ENVIRONMENT
IS YOUR FOOD NUTRITIOUS?

Are you getting the recommended amounts of vitamins and nutrition in your diet?

The answer is probably no! The American diet is badly out of balance and does not supply the needed nutrition. For the last 30 or 40 years, our food has been processed in hydrogenated oils, butter and fats and loaded with chemicals and preservatives to the point of making it poor nutritionally.

"Nutritional deficiency is made worse by poor food choices that overload diet with empty calories high in fat, sugar, and processed starch from rice, corn, wheat, and oats," Dr. Ringsdorf says.

The wheat in flour has been processed so much it has lost its nutritional value, even though some vitamins are added to it. That's why I prefer not to eat bread with this program.

In some countries fresh, whole grains ground and baked into bread the day you buy and eat them. However, finding whole grain bread without preservatives unless you make it yourself is very difficult in the United States.

AMERICAN DIET IS VERY POOR
TAKE SUPPLEMENTS

In my opinion we process, add preservatives and handle food too much. Keeping your body healthy by what you eat is impossible. You must have supplements.

Dr. Sheldon S. Hendler, a member of the medical school faculty at the University of California, San Diego, said in <u>The Doctors' Vitamin and Mineral Encyclopedia</u> (Fireside/Simon & Schuster, 1990) that "the `Great American diet,' far from providing optimal nutrition, has just about done us in." He explained the American diet is full of nutritional imbalances and deficiencies. Dr. Hendler advised taking vitamin supplements.

Today, few people even eat regularly and even fewer eat the government-recommended three balanced meals per day. A national government survey showed out of 22,000 people in the survey, not one person received 100 percent of the Recommended Daily Allowance (RDA) for the ten necessary nutrients from diet alone.

See the end of Chapter 6 for the list of suggested supplements. Remember to take supplements with a meal for best absorption of the nutrients. At a meal, the body is already primed to transport food through the body. The food's enzymes are released, and the blood is flowing to move the vitamins through your body.

POLLUTION AND SAFE FOODS

Processed foods and chemical pollutants in that food as well as our poor eating habits all contribute to nutrition deficiencies. What can you do about it?

If you are a farmer or have a vegetable garden, you know how much better fresh vegetables taste. Vegetables are better when grown the old way with natural fertilizers and mulch to enrich the soil. Not only are they tastier, they are more nutritious.

Have your own garden if possible, or buy from stores with fresh, safe vegetables. The fresher the fruit or vegetable, then the less it has been handled and the more nutritious it will be.

You will find less nutrition in your food because of:
* bruising of fruit and vegetables,
* handling food too much,
* buying old and/or wilted fruit and vegetables and
* refrigerating improperly.

Include only the freshest fruit and vegetables in your diet to get the most nutrition. Eat the whole fruit and vegetable — skin and all. Nutrients usually are concentrated in the outer layer of a plant. Also, remember raw nuts have more thiamine and vitamin B-6 than roasted nuts. Also eat unprocessed brown rice and whole grain bread, if you can find it. Use whole grain flour, and bake your own bread when you have time for a true flavor.

Store your produce whole. Cut produce in big chunks just before you plan to eat. The smaller you cut fruits or vegetables, more vitamins are destroyed by oxidation. Refrigerate fresh greens in an airtight container. If you use a plastic bag, punch a hole in the bag for proper drainage.

AVOID FOOD POISONING

Protect your family from food poisoning and salmonella. You'll know if you have it within one to six hours after eating. The intense nausea, diarrhea, vomiting and fever should be over within a day or two. If you feel bad for more than two days, call your doctor because food poisoning can be fatal. If you think you got the food poisoning from a restaurant or through eating store-bought processed food, call the health department.

You can kill most bacteria at a temperature of 165 degrees Fahrenheit (F) or below 40 degrees F. Always keep your food either hot or cold. Bacteria can multiply fast. Mayonnaise and products containing eggs are particularly susceptible to spoiling quickly.

When you have picnics or family get-togethers, put the food up or on ice as soon as everyone is served. Going back for thirds of Aunt Tilley's warm potato salad has put many a good man down.

You must cook all meat and seafood thoroughly. Also, poultry and raw eggs often are contaminated with salmonella. You must clean these foods carefully and cook them thoroughly. When cooking poultry, you must maintain an internal temperature of 170 degrees F for at least half an hour.

Keep your hands, knives and cutting board very clean. Wash your hands often. Clean your refrigerator regularly. Throw away food that has started to mold (except cheese) before it contaminates other food.

Preventing food poisoning is not difficult. Think ahead and keep your family healthier.

DEAD SOIL AND CHEMICAL FERTILIZERS

Soil that is fertilized chemically often is dead soil. It is easy to overfertilize with chemicals. You'll find the lively, microbial organisms that make the soil active and healthy are dead, and the soil is dry and usually hard-packed. Plants then have only chemicals for food. Chemically prepared fertilizers may produce a big crop, but this produce isn't worth much to the human body.

Too, the chemicals will run off into the water supply and cause further damage and pollution to the environment and the food chain. Using chemical fertilizers in a garden has been shown to be no more productive than when gardeners utilized manure and organic methods to fertilize and keep pests under control.

LOSS OF TOPSOIL

An alarming report from the United Nations stated that since 1945, mankind has damaged more than one-tenth of the Earth's fertile soil, which is an area the size of China and India combined. The loss of fertile topsoil is a threat to the whole world's food supply, since this soil is the only place we have to grow food.

Many reasons are given for the loss of the Earth's topsoil. In Alabama where I live, and the South in general, poor farming and forestry practices like improper clear-cutting cause soil to wash away. Overgrazing, the growth of cities, and pollution like acid rain also are to blame.

MANY MEDICINES ARE LOST
AS FORESTS ARE CUT

Scientists at the National Cancer Institute are studying plants to find cures for cancer. They have identified 3,000 plants as possible cancer cures. Seventy percent of those are found in tropical rain forests. Much more is at stake than just the loss of our forests and topsoil if we continue to utilize poor farming and forestry practices.

We must all be partners in the conservation of our resources. We can do something about this problem. We also can work together to improve water quality and eliminate air and noise pollution as well as other problems with our environment.

LIMITED WATER SUPPLY AND AIR POLLUTION

Even though most of our planet's surface is water, only less than one percent is safe to drink. Since our bodies are made mostly of water—about 70 percent—fresh water is of prime importance to our survival. Yet we have allowed much of our water supply to be contaminated by agricultural and industrial practices and man's old enemies: viruses, bacteria and fungi.

The groundwater in 30 states was found to be contaminated by more than 60 pesticides in a study by the

EPA in 1988. Estimates from public and private studies show that as much as 37 percent of our public drinking water supplies is contaminated with toxic or bacterial contaminants.

The pollution in our air also gets in our groundwater. We must deal with car and industrial emissions if we are to do anything about cleaning up our water. Lead and other heavy metals come from our cars' exhausts.

The government's standards for drinking water allow for a maximum contaminant level. These standards are controversial because not enough is known about how small amounts of toxins affect our health. Many of these toxins build up over time in our bodies and cause diseases that are hard to trace back to toxins in water. Because only a fixed amount of water is on Earth, we must work together to protect and clean up our water and air.

CHEMICALS AND POISONS IN OUR FOOD

Chemical agriculture includes fertilizers and pesticides that have destroyed the soil's critically important microbial life. These chemicals include fungicides, insecticides and herbicides.

This information is alarming, folks, since these chemicals are also regularly found in the food we buy at the grocery stores. We are eating the same chemicals we feed our plants and the poisons we use to kill their pests.

CHEMICALS ADDED TO FOOD

Consider that these chemicals and poisons are in addition to the chemicals already added to our foods, including artificial colors, artificial flavors and preservatives. These chemicals are in most of our foods and goods bought in the grocery store. Many of these additions to our food are suspected of causing cancer.

Drugs and hormones fed to livestock remain in the animals' bodies and are eaten by us when we eat meat. This problem is particularly suspect in large animals like cows. That's another reason I don't eat red meat.

Since most chickens and turkeys are not raised with hormones, they usually are safe to eat. Always cook poultry without the skin, or remove the skin when you dine out.

"LADIES AND GENTLEMEN, THIS IS OUR NEWEST PRODUCT. IT IS ABSOLUTELY WORTHLESS AS A FOOD_ BUT WE'LL PUT ON OUR MOST EXPENSIVE AND ELABORATE TV AND PRINT MEDIA BLITZ EVER... AND THE PUBLIC WILL BE CRYING FOR IT ! "

OCEAN POLLUTION

The oceans around the United States as well as our lakes and streams are polluted by farming, industrial chemicals, and sewage waste. Be careful where you get your fish and seafood. Farm-raised catfish should be safe if prepared properly.

Fish caught far from our shore are safer than those caught near land. I read a report recently that says the safest seafood comes from Mexico, Argentina, Chile and New Zealand. Check at your super market to learn where the seafood has come from before you buy it.

If you want to learn more about getting safe food for your family, read these books, which I highly recommend: Diet For A Poisoned Planet by David Steinman (Harmony Books/New York 1990) and The Bread & Circus Whole Food Bible (Addison Wesley/New York 1991).

TOO MANY OF US

Everybody is becoming more and more aware that too many people live on Earth. Experts say the world's population will double in about 50 years with the population growing from 5.5 billion to over 10 billion by the year 2050. This information is frightening for our children and grandchildren and has far-reaching implications.

If you are a hunter or a fisherman as I am, you have noticed how our forests are disappearing, and many of our streams are muddy and dead. Have you ever wondered what happens to the animals, the birds, the squirrels and the rabbits as well as the deer when we clear-cut forests? Well, they die of starvation or stress-related illnesses like heart attacks.

This same crowding causes humans to suffer stress-related diseases. What can you do about it? In my opinion, you will give your children a better chance at a good life and help the planet if you limit your family to two children.

Another thing you can do is teach our young people about birth control and the importance of having the ability to care for the children they do choose to have. In some countries, families spend 80 percent of their incomes for food to feed their large families. Two good books are Your Complete Guide To Sexual Health by Elizabeth Thompson Ortiz and Our Bodies, Ourselves by the Boston Women's Health Book Collective.

ALUMINUM TOXICITY

Another controversy that only lately has received the research attention it deserves is the effects of the accumulation of aluminum on the body. Aluminum is one of the most common metals on Earth and is found in the soil, the air, the water and our food in small amounts.

The symptoms of aluminum poisoning include anemia, headache, colic, gastrointestinal disturbances, decreased liver and kidney function, memory loss, forgetfulness, extreme nervousness, speech disturbances, bone softening and weak muscles.

An excess of aluminum interferes with calcium metabolism. Poor calcium metabolism can cause chronic calcium deficiencies that may keep your body from properly using minerals.

Many of these symptoms are found in patients with Alzheimer's disease and osteoporosis. Aluminum toxicity is highly suspected as causes of these diseases.

Aluminum is found in a surprising number of over-the-counter drugs. The most common cause of toxicity is the excessive use of antacids, which contain aluminum hydroxide. Aluminum is found in other drugs, including those taken for inflammation and pain, some douches and also in most baking powders.

Aluminum is found in antiperspirants, pickles, table salt, grated cheese, canned goods and processed cheese. Some evidence supports the idea that cooking with aluminum pots, pans, cooking utensils and foil also can contribute to aluminum toxicity. You may want to cook in stainless steel, glass or iron cookware.

What can you do? Try to avoid aluminum as much as possible by reading labels and increasing your awareness of where you come in contact with aluminum. A high-fiber diet like the one I've outlined will help your body eliminate many toxins.

DEADLY CAMPER COVERS

I just want to caution parents who put their children in the backs of their trucks inside camper covers. Many children have died of inhaling poisonous gases from the truck's exhaust. The gases get inside the cover and suffocate children.

Long trips are more suspect. But even short trips can hurt your family. If your kids complain of headaches and get car-sick when they ride in back, you may have a serious problem. A little precaution now can stop a terrible tragedy later.

If you are accustomed to traveling this way with your family, please check to be sure the exhaust is diverted to the side and cannot get blown back into the camper. Make sure that side windows don't suck the gases inside.

A LESS STRESSFUL ENVIRONMENT

My life is complicated, and I know yours is, too. Not only am I busy, but I have to deal with traffic, deadlines, trying to keep myself and my family happy, noise pollution, air pollution and much more. All these things are stressful.

Stress affects practically every organ in the body. It can make any disease or illness much worse and slows down your immune system.

SHARE YOUR LIFE WITH FRIENDS

Don't let stress build up. Take time to relax and enjoy life. Show and share love. Spend time with your family, friends and pets. Laugh a lot. Invest the time required to keep good friends.

"Laughter is the best medicine" is an old but very true saying. And sharing a laugh with good friends is the best.

PETS CAN REDUCE STRESS

Studies show having pets drastically can reduce stress. They are loving and don't demand more time than you can give. The time you spend in caring for a pet can be just as relaxing as the time you spend playing with them. Walking your dog can be the best way to be sure you exercise every day.

Sometimes you can talk to your pet about things you can't tell anyone else. Start talking to your family, too. People seem to talk more if a pet is around, even if they just exchange pet stories.

TAKE AN EXERCISE BREAK

If things pile up at work or home and you find you are ready to lose your temper, take a little break. Get off by yourself. Go for a walk outside or up and down the stairs. A good yawn and a stretch really relieves tension.

JOIN A SPORTS TEAM, TAKE VACATIONS

If you enjoy a team sport, find some folks you can play with, because the exercise and the friendship can't be beat. Square dancing, bopping and other dancing is good group exercise, too.

Plan to get away from all your responsibilities often. Take short weekend vacations as well as a two-week vacation every year.

TAKE TIME FOR YOURSELF

Keep the Bible or an inspirational book with you to read and lift your spirits. Prayer or meditation can nip anxiety and stress in the bud.

If you leave ten minutes earlier for work, you will have a chance to plan your day and have a minute to yourself. Take breaks often, and walk around and stretch your body.

Slow down. Why hurry everywhere? Your life is happening now — not in thirty minutes when you get

TIME FOR DECISION

somewhere. A relaxing drive home will put you in the mood for family and friends.

MAKE NEW FRIENDS

Get to know the people you work with as well as your neighbors, fellow church members and family. Sharing your life with others helps more than you'll ever know. Friendship and love are the best medicines you can use.

Of course, eating right, having healthy sleep habits and getting proper exercise are also very important in handling the stresses of life. Develop a positive healthy attitude about everything you do. Learn to relax.

REMEMBER

o   Take vitamin supplements with your meals because the American diet is poor nutritionally.

o   Use care in handling your food to keep it nutritious. o   Avoid getting food poisoning.

o   Share in caring for our environment: the air, water, forests and topsoil.

o   Avoid processed food.

o   Eat fresh raw food without chemicals. o   Don't overcook meat and other foods.

o   Be aware of where your food comes from to avoid pesticides and other chemicals.

o   Make your life as stress-free as possible.

o   Develop a positive, healthy attitude.

o   Learn to relax.

o   Cultivate friendship and love, which are the best medicines.

Chapter 13

WHAT ABOUT DIABETES?

I want to say something about diabetes in case you are not familiar with the condition. I didn't know much about it until I was told I had it. Then I found out everything I could about this serious problem affecting so many Americans.

Diabetes is a serious but treatable condition. I'm not going to try to give a detailed explanation of diabetes but here is a brief definition.

The diabetic's body cannot make full use of some of the foods eaten, mainly carbohydrates or sugars and starches. In a healthy person's body, simple and complex carbohydrates are converted to glucose. However, in the diabetic, instead of a smooth conversion, the blood sugar will swing wildly. Sometimes the blood sugar level will be very high like mine was and then later drop way low.

A hormone called insulin is needed for the body to use and store glucose. Insulin also regulates the amount of glucose in the bloodstream. In a diabetic, either not enough insulin is present or the body is not able to use insulin properly.

The sudden highs and lows will finally overwork the pancreas. Then the pancreas won't know what to do. The pancreas' job is to make enough insulin available to burn food as energy or store the energy for future use.

The pancreas is a large gland lying across and behind the stomach. It also produces pancreatic enzymes, which help digest the proteins, fats and carbohydrates in food.

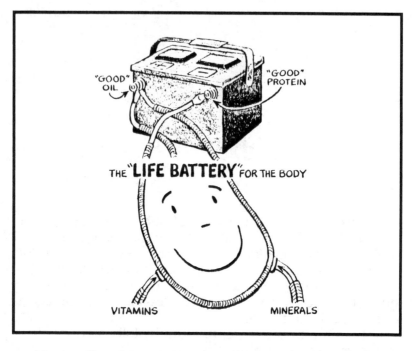

THE "LIFE BATTERY" FOR THE BODY

"GOOD" OIL

"GOOD" PROTEIN

VITAMINS

MINERALS

Normally the excess carbohydrate energy is converted to a form of sugar called glycogen, which is stored in the liver and muscles. Starches and sugars increase the blood sugar content. Any excess sugar passes through the kidneys and into the urine.

In a diabetic's body, too much of the carbohydrate energy is lost through urine. When this problem occurs, the body begins to break down its own fat and protein in an attempt to provide needed energy. This breaking down causes dangerous acidic toxins to form, which causes acidosis or ketosis in the blood. This condition can be life-threatening. Sugar can kill a diabetic.

When the body starts to run out of gasoline, it knows the only way to get blood sugar is to eat. A diabetic must watch carbohydrate intake carefully and eat more complex carbohydrates. He should eat small meals all day long, usually from six to twelve little meals.

Most people will eat a sugar product when their energy level drops — cookies, cake, candy bar or anything sweet, which will kick the energy level up quickly. But a diabetic can get in serious trouble and even die if he or she does this. Every time the energy level kicks up with sugar, it drops fast again.

Although this yo-yo effect is rough on a healthy person, a diabetic may lose consciousness or experience worse problems. The more severe diabetics must inject themselves once or twice daily with insulin to keep from having these highs and lows.

A diabetic needs to eat complex carbohydrates like those found in fresh fruits, vegetables, beans and natural whole grains. Complex carbohydrates also add fiber to your diet and have one-third the calories found in fat and simple carbohydrates like sugar. The complex carbohydrates convert to fat and are burned slowly to provide long-term energy.

EAT LESS PROTEIN AND FAT

Too much protein will overstimulate and thus overwork the pancreas, which is another reason to eat more complex carbohydrates. Too much protein, especially animal protein, causes the pancreas to excrete excess pancreatic enzyme. You don't want to waste this important cancer-fighting enzyme by eating too much protein.

Saturated fat like that found in meat also interferes with the metabolism of insulin. Several studies have shown that fewer vegetarians have diabetes then non-vegetarians. The fact that meat eaters consume a lower amount of complex carbohydrates and fiber also may contribute to a higher risk of getting diabetes.

The high levels of sugar in the diabetic's blood cause a deficiency in the essential fatty acid, linoleic acid, by making the linoleic acid in the fat tissues unavailable to the body. Diabetics must eat foods high in linoleic acid like flax seeds, soybeans, pumpkin seeds, walnuts, salmon, mackerel, rainbow trout, sardines and whole grains. (See Chapter 10 for more information on essential fatty acids).

The pancreas is the most important organ in the body to prevent disease. Don't mess it up. To keep your pancreas healthy, cut down on protein and saturated fat and eliminate sugar.

HOW DO YOU GET DIABETES?

Over five million diabetics are in the United States. Some researchers believe people who have diabetes get it through inheritance. This theory emphasizes that people who are most likely to develop diabetes are ones who are overweight and over 40 years of age and are related to a diabetic.

Other researchers believe that diabetes is a fatty degeneration disease that is the result of the consumption of the wrong fats and refined sugars and starches and is associated with a diet severely deficient in vitamins and minerals.

Major risk factors include having the disease in the family, obesity and advanced age. More people in certain ethnic groups are affected. If you are Hispanic, Native American or a African American, you are at a greater risk for developing diabetes. If you are at risk, take charge right now. Get to work to prevent getting the disease.

Diabetics are one of two types: insulin-dependent or Type I and non-insulin-dependent or Type II. About 80 percent of diabetics are Type II. They produce insulin but not enough to keep their blood sugar in the normal range.

Symptoms include increased thirst, constant hunger, frequent urination, loss of weight, itching especially around the groin, marked fatigue, high blood pressure, changes in vision and cuts and scratches that are slow to heal. See your doctor right away if you suspect you may be a diabetic.

GET OFF CAFFEINE

People with diabetes should not drink coffee and high-caffeine sodas. Folks drink coffee all day because the caffeine kicks up their blood sugar levels. But when the blood sugar crashes, they experience terrible lows — usually in the late afternoon. Then they feel terrible. The more caffeine you drink, the harder your pancreas must work.

EXERCISE TO AVOID TYPE II DIABETES

As I mentioned in Chapter 4, exercise has been shown to possibly prevent non-insulin dependent Type II diabetes in people who are at risk for the disease. Exercise

"THE DOCTOR OF THE FUTURE WILL GIVE NO MEDICINE BUT WILL INTEREST HIS PATIENTS IN THE CARE OF THE HUMAN FRAME, IN DIET, AND IN THE CAUSE AND PREVENTION OF DISEASE."

Thomas Alva Edison — 1847-1931

has been used successfully for many years to manage those patients who already have this form of diabetes.

If you are at risk or already have diabetes, talk to your doctor. Plan a reasonable exercise program. I exercise regularly and feel this exercise helps me control my diabetes. Besides, the exercise helps me keep off the 80 pounds I lost and makes me feel good.

HYPOGLYCEMIA

Here's another caution. If you are having trouble with low blood sugar, see your doctor now for a complete checkup. Some very serious conditions can cause these

113

symptoms, including liver disease, cancer, tumors of the beta cells, underactive adrenal or pituitary glands, starvation or alcoholism.

The symptoms of hypoglycemia include fatigue or unusual tiredness, weakness, nervousness, an unusual amount of sweating and irritability. Hypoglycemia can sometimes cause fainting and, although rarely even loss of consciousness. These symptoms usually disappear when the affected person eats some food.

DANGER — DIABETICS AND LOW BLOOD SUGAR

Low blood sugar can be very serious for a diabetic, too. A hypoglycemic reaction will come on very suddenly and must be treated quickly. Orange juice, a cola, two lumps of sugar or seven or eight Lifesaver mints will bring a diabetic out of this situation. If not, you should get medical help immediately.

NORMAL LIFESTYLE

Diabetes is a serious but treatable disease. If you find you have it, then learn as much as you can about it. Be an active patient. Make a commitment to yourself to stay as healthy as possible. Keep your weight down. Stay active.

With the new knowledge about how nutrition and exercise affect diabetes, a diabetic can live a well-rounded lifestyle. The home blood sugar test I told you about in Chapter 3 can give the diabetic immediate and accurate information on blood sugar levels and allows the diabetic to regulate his food intake or insulin intake at the most effective level.

Diabetics live full, happy lives. They marry, have kids and work in every type of job or career. They are athletes, scientists, artists, carpenters, mechanics and doctors from all walks of life. Some famous diabetics include Elvis Presley, Mary Tyler Moore, Thomas Edison, Howard Hughes and Jackie Robinson.

If you become a member of the American Diabetes Association, you can receive the "Diabetes Forecast" and join a local chapter for lots of support. The address is 1660 Duke Street, Alexandria, VA 22314. There are several other good magazines available to diabetics. I particularly

114

like "Diabetes Self-Management." The address is P.O. Box 51125, Boulder, CO 80321-1125.

Many good books on diabetes are available. I recommend these two:

A Diabetic Doctor Looks At Diabetes by Peter A. Lodewick, M.D., R.M.I. Corporation, Massachusetts, 1988

Diabetes: A Guide To Living Well by Ernest Lowe & Gary Arsham, M.D., Ph.D, Diabetes Center, Inc., publisher, 1989.

These two cookbooks are especially helpful:

Cookbook for Diabetics and Their Families by UAB Department of Dietetics, Oxmoor House, Inc., Alabama, 1986

Recipes for Diabetics by Billie Little, Perigee Books · Putnam Publishing, New York, 1981.

REMEMBER

o   Act now to prevent developing diabetes if you are at risk.

o   Keep your weight down.

o   Eat more carbohydrates and fiber foods.

o   Eat less protein.

o   Give up caffeine.

o   Eat foods high in the essential fatty acids, like flax seeds, soybeans, walnuts, fish and whole grains.

o   Exercise.

o   Keep a healthy attitude.

o   See your doctor immediately if you think you have a problem with hypoglycemia (low blood sugar).

o   Be an active patient.

o   Work hard to stay as healthy as possible.

o   Learn all about the disease, and keep up with new information.

o   Remember diabetes is a serious but treatable disease.

Chapter 14

A HEALTHY HEART

I don't need to tell you how important your heart is. But keeping your heart healthy takes work. Your heart pumps about 2,000 gallons of blood through about 70,000 miles of blood vessels each day at 40 miles per hour. Heart disease is the number one killer in the United States, killing almost one in every two Americans.

Modern medicine now has discovered that most cases of heart disease can be prevented. The top three heart threats are high cholesterol, high blood pressure and smoking. All of these problems can be controlled.

If we control what we eat, we can control our cholesterol levels. We also can help control our blood pressure by eating right, exercising and taking medication. The third bad heart threat is smoking cigarettes. Just stop smoking, and that's that.

Some other problems can contribute to heart problems, but they, too, can be controlled. They include not exercising and sitting around too much (like in front of the TV), being overweight, letting yourself worry too much, getting angry or being hostile all the time and, of course, my problem, diabetes.

CHOLESTEROL

I'm sure you have probably read about the problems cholesterol causes your heart and circulation. What is cholesterol? Cholesterol is necessary to all our cells. It is white and sticky, not a fat but more wax-like, tasteless and odorless. It is the raw material that makes cell membranes, bile acids and sex hormones.

We get cholesterol from the food we eat and from our own intestinal tracts and our livers. If you eat food with high amounts of cholesterol, then your body makes less. If you eat too little, the body makes more. A diet high in non-essential fatty acids and refined carbohydrates, like sugar and white flour, causes the body to increase cholesterol production. (See Chapter 10 on Fats).

The problem with too much cholesterol is it can build up on the inside walls of the blood vessels that are like tunnels through which the blood flows. It also can build up inside the heart and the arteries that pump the blood to the heart.

In bad cases, the walls of blood vessels become so blocked they harden. Then the flow of nutrients and blood is slowed or stopped. The heart can't work right. One symptom is severe pain called angina in the chest or the left side or arm. Heart disease has three different names: coronary artery disease, cardiovascular disease and CHD.

GOOD AND BAD CHOLESTEROL

Good and bad cholesterol are present in our bodies. Reducing the bad cholesterol level leads to a healthier heart and can reverse the effects of the disease. The low-density-lipo-protein (LDL) cholesterol is bad because it is the one that clogs your arteries.

High-density-lipo-protein (HDL) cholesterol, on the other hand, is the good one since it will pass through your arteries and doesn't stick to them.

To maintain high levels of the good HDL and low levels of the bad LDL, you must receive less than 20 percent of your food calories from fat. Most people receive 40 percent or more calories from fat. Your cholesterol level should be between 160 and 200 mg/dl.

Saturated fat is the key bad guy. Don't fry anything ever again, and avoid all hydrogenated oils like margarine. Animal fat is high in saturated fat. That's why I suggest cutting out red meat and always skinning any poultry. Use unsaturated fats. Some of the best are flax seed, safflower, and corn oil. (See Chapter 10 on Fats for more information).

KEEPS IT SOARING

Eat more fish. The omega-3 fatty acids in fish oils seem to change the way cholesterol is deposited. A study in the New England Journal of Medicine in 1985 showed that men who ate three ounces of fish each week had a 36 percent lower death rate from heart disease then men who ate no fish.

Another substance found in oily fish like sardines and mackerel, as well as produced in the body, is coenzyme Q. Coenzyme Q, a powerful antioxidant, helps prevent dangerous LDL cholesterol from damaging your arteries.

Interestingly, if you cut your cholesterol number by 1 percent, you reduce your odds of getting heart disease by 2 percent. You also can slow aging by keeping your cholesterol under 200 mg/dl. You can have the arteries of a 50-year-old at age 70.

Take everyone in your family to have their cholesterol levels checked. Even children may have problems with high cholesterol. The diet I've recommended is low in fat and cholesterol.

HIGH BLOOD PRESSURE

High blood pressure or hypertension is a problem for an estimated 40 million Americans. Many thousands of people die needlessly from this problem every year when all they needed to do is follow well-known treatment.

High blood pressure means the heart has abnormally high pressure as it pumps blood through arteries and presses against blood vessels. The heart has to work harder than it should, which can lead to heart failure and stroke.

Because high blood pressure often has no noticeable symptoms, you need to have a thorough check-up with your doctor regularly. You are at risk for high blood pressure if you are overweight or have a family history of hypertension.

Often high blood pressure is caused by cigarette smoking, stress, obesity, excessive use of stimulants like coffee or soft drinks, drug abuse, high sodium (salt) intake and use of oral contraceptives. Alcohol also makes blood pressure rise when the equivalent of four or more beers are drunk in a day. Cut any or all of these out, and often your blood pressure will fall on its own.

Another cause of high blood pressure is arteriosclerosis or hardening of the arteries. The blood vessels and arteries become constricted with cholesterol plaque and cause blood pressure to go up.

NON-DRUG TREATMENT TO LOWER PRESSURE

Many people with high blood pressure are helped by certain doctor-prescribed drugs. Non-drug treatment like the way of life I've outlined sometimes can control mild high blood pressure and reduce the amount of drugs

KEEPS THE MEMBRANES OF OUR CELLS FUNCTIONING PROPERLY

PROTECTS SKIN FROM CRACKING, DEHYDRATION, AND WEAR AND TEAR OF THE SUN AND WATER

MAKES THE STEROID HORMONES

HELPS IN HEALING SKIN TISSUE

PREVENTS FOREIGN ORGANISMS FROM INFECTING THE SKIN

MAKES IT EASIER TO DIGEST FOOD FATS

"GOOD" CHOLESTEROL

needed in severe cases. Remain under a doctor's care to keep your blood pressure under control.

To lower blood pressure, a salt-free diet is absolutely necessary. Read labels. Avoid anything with soda, sodium or the symbol Na on it. Just about everything can have some salt in it. Remember that chewing tobacco and snuff are loaded with sodium.

Eat foods high in fiber. Fiber aids digestion and helps rid your body of toxins. Also load up on calcium to help lower your blood pressure.

Research by James H. Dwyer of the USC School of Medicine in Los Angeles has shown that calcium helps reduce high blood pressure. A deficiency in calcium may even cause high blood pressure. Take 1,500 to 3,000 mg every day. You also may need to increase your potassium and magnesium.

You'll need to keep your weight down and exercise regularly. But avoid over-exercising and emotional stress. Also, stop taking antihistamines unless your doctor tells you to take them. Too vigorous sex may be dangerous.

This condition can be very serious, folks. Have your blood pressure checked at least four times a year if you have a risk for high blood pressure.

OATS AND LEMONS CLEAN BLOOD VESSELS

When you first start off life, you'll have nice, clean blood vessels. However, over time all the junk, heavy metals, fat, and cholesterol start sticking on the inside of those vessels. We live in a hostile environment. We can't get rid of the lead and other pollution in the air we breathe.

Over time, poisons pile up in our vessels. Our bodies know to go ahead and crust over these substances to keep them from floating around inside. But then our blood vessels start narrowing down from the crusts, and the blood can't flow through like it needs to for good health.

What can you do? Although the idea may sound crazy, you can "rotor rooter" your blood vessels by using chelation therapy, a process to clean the blood vessels.

You'll find the history of chelation very interesting. Back in the 1930s, people often worked in lead factories and got lead poisoning, a very serious and deadly disease. Doctors invented ethylene-diamine-tetra-acetic acid (EDTA) that they put through the sick workers' blood vessels.

This particular material, EDTA, had an affinity for lead. Molecularly the lead would come out of the vessel walls, stick tightly to the EDTA and get in the bloodstream. Then away it would go to be cleaned out of the body.

Six to eight months later, the people who had other kinds of problems like high blood pressure, diabetes, and low blood sugar found their symptoms had gotten better or gone away. The molecular action from the EDTA was cleaning out the blood vessels and allowing the blood to flow strong again, making these people healthier.

Lemons and oats can do the same thing. As they go through your system molecularly, they start pulling out the fatty tissues and other poisonous stuff, and slowly but surely your blood vessels will clear up.

BYPASSING BYPASS SURGERY

One of the most interesting books you'll ever want to read is Bypassing the Bypass by Dr. Elmer Cranton and Arline Brecher (Medex, Virginia 1984). Dr. Canton shows how the enzymes and the proper foods go to work to clean out your body.

When surgeons perform bypass surgery, they clean vessels only near your heart. You still have about another 70 thousand miles of vessels and arteries in your body with some so small that one cell must bend to pass through them.

Because of the limited work of bypass surgery, I wasn't surprised by the results of one study. On one group, doctors performed bypass surgery and on the other group doctors provided no treatment. The results were exactly the same except one group spent $50,000 on a blood vessel operation and the other group didn't.

If you have a bucket of muddy water and you want to clean it, you can take the whole bucket and dump it out. Or, you can put a hose in a bucket and let the clean water run into the muddy water and eventually purge the mud out. Of course you can't throw the body away if you want to clean it. However, you can try to purge the muddy water out of the body with the proper foods. Chelation is very important because it is done after these foods have been ingested and takes the junk out.

Once you've tried to live a healthier lifestyle by following the suggestions in this book for several months, you'll find you feel so much better. You'll have much more zip and you'll get more enjoyment out of your life.

HEART-HEALTHY FOOD

Some foods and ways of preparing foods are better for you than others. Heart-healthy foods help decrease your cholesterol levels help prevent heart attacks and may help your arthritis and joint problems.

Fish is a heart-healthy food. Eat fish at least three times a week. Like other people interested in good health, I also take one cod liver oil tablet every day.

Recent research at the University of Wisconsin Medical School found that red grape juice helps prevent the formation of blood clots, which can cause heart attacks. The red grape juice contains natural substances called flavonoids, which have anti-clotting properties.

Green, leafy vegetables, oranges, dried beans and other foods rich in folic acid also help prevent heart attacks, Folic acid helps defuse homocysteine, an amino acid in the blood that is a villain in heart disease. Harvard researchers say 150,000 heart attacks annually are tied to high levels of blood homocysteine.

Soybeans are a really healthy, low-fat source of complete protein and is the mainstay of most vegetarians' diets. You can find tofu, a good source of soybeans, in either the fresh vegetable or the dairy section of the grocery store. Some research has shown that soybeans may help pre-cancerous cells recover and become normal again.

LOWER YOUR BLOOD PRESSURE
AND CHOLESTEROL

Oranges are high in vitamin C and also contain a high amount of D-glucarate. Oranges will help reduce your

125

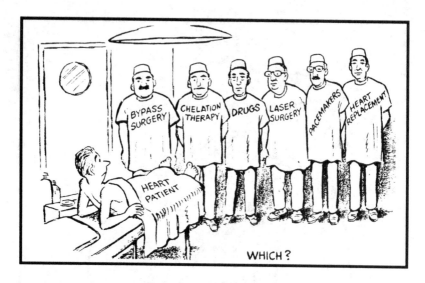

WHICH?

blood cholesterol and fight plaque in your arteries. Oranges also combat some viruses. Other foods that contain D-glucarate include apples, cherries, bean sprouts, potatoes and broccoli. See Chapter 9 for more about D-glucarate.

Calcium has been shown to lower blood pressure as well as build strong bones. Low-fat yogurt is a great source of calcium.

Garlic, onions, leeks, shallots and chives have been shown to fight colds and may be able to lower blood cholesterol levels. Garlic eaten raw stimulates the immune system. Onions contain quercetin, which may block the formation of tumors, especially in the stomach.

Gelatin and pectin-rich fruits like apples, plums and pears also have been shown to lower cholesterol. Dried beans, dried peas and lentils are all high-protein, low-fat legumes that can help lower blood cholesterol.

FIGHT HEART DISEASE AND STROKE

The oriental shitake mushroom acts as an anti-coagulant that may prevent the risk of heart disease and stroke. It also has a virus-fighting substance called lentinan.

Potassium can aid in preventing strokes. Good sources of potassium are potatoes with their skins,

Brussels sprouts, broccoli, mushrooms, parsnips, parsley, avocados, plums, bananas and apples.

HEART-HEALTHY SUPPLEMENTS

Niacin can help lower dangerous LDL cholesterol levels and raise good HDL levels. Most researchers suggest a supplement of 3 grams daily, but even 1 gram daily can help cholesterol levels. However, your liver might not be able to handle the added burden of niacin metabolism, and side effects may include blurred vision, nausea and vomiting. Be sure to have your liver function tested two to three months after beginning niacin supplements.

Niacin is not recommended for people with active peptic ulcer, liver disease, severe heart arrhythmias, diabetes or gout; or people who are heavy drinkers.

Melatonin, another antioxidant that helps prevent artery damage, is a natural hormone in the body. Studies have found people with very high blood pressure have lower levels of melatonin than those with moderate hypertension. So supplementing your diet with melatonin can help your heart stay healthy.

STRESS CAN CONTRIBUTE TO HEART DISEASE

Don't let stress ruin your health. Be in charge of your life.

Learn to be sensitive to yourself. Don't let things build up; put first things first; don't rush to each new demand; and, most importantly, take time to relax. Your life depends on it. I've discussed stress in greater detail in Chapter 10.

HEART-HEALTHY EXERCISE

Exercise benefits your heart and lungs and probably is the best thing you can do for your heart. To shape up, you need to raise your heart rate for at least 20 minutes a minimum of three times a week and preferably five times a week.

I have covered exercise in Chapter 4. Remember, check with your doctor before you launch into a vigorous exercise program. If you've been a couch potato, you'll need supervising to get a healthy exercise program started.

Build up slowly. Forget the saying "no pain, no gain." Pain is only for professional athletes. Enjoy getting your body toned. Since exercise is the best thing you can do for a healthy heart, get started.

REMEMBER:

o   A healthy heart can be yours.
o   You must stop smoking.
o   Keep your cholesterol below 200 mg/dl.
o   You must avoid getting high blood pressure or keep it under control by eating right, keeping your weight down and exercising.
o   You can help clean out your system by eating lemons and oats.
o   You can perhaps bypass bypass surgery by taking care of yourself and using chelation therapy.
o   You need to eat heart-healthy food.
o   You must avoid stress and exercise regularly.

Chapter 15

GOOD HEALTH IS YOUR JOB

I want to cover some important information that will help you become healthier. Your good health is your job, your responsibility. You don't know how good you can feel until you set a goal of becoming as healthy as possible. Believing in yourself is magic.

QUIT SMOKING

"Cigarette smoking is the chief, single, avoidable cause of death in our society and the most important public health issue of our time," former Surgeon General Koop said while he was in office. This statement is still true.

Smokers may get the same kind of heart disease that attacks diabetics because of sugars in tobacco that form a "molecular glue" and harden arteries, Anthony Cerami of the Picower Institute for Medical Research found in a study. Cerami also discovered that chemicals in cigarettes reduce the blood's ability to carry oxygen and force the heart to pump harder and cause blood clots.

If you smoke, the best thing you can do for your health is to quit. Each year nearly 400,000 Americans die premature deaths directly linked to smoking, which is more than those killed in car accidents or by alcohol, cocaine, heroin and AIDS combined.

Thirty out of every 100 deaths this year will be from smoking. The number of cigarette-related deaths are going up for women. Women must not smoke at all if they are pregnant or have small children. Smoking related deaths are the leading cause of death for men ages 35-69.

WE'RE DEPENDING ON **THEM** TO DO **OUR** JOB

Secondhand smoke from cigarettes also affects the health of your family and friends. You will help them by quitting. The Environmental Protection Agency in early 1993 labeled secondhand smoke a carcinogen. Studies have found that a minimum of 5,000 people develop lung cancer each year because of secondhand smoke.

Dr. James Pirkle of The Centers for Disease Control and Prevention in Atlanta is the director of a federal study of 23,000 Americans over age four to detect cotinine, a by-product of nicotine found in the blood. Of the first 800 people tested, all showed some cotinine in the blood, which is a greater than 60 to 70 percent increase over figures gathered in smaller studies of cotinine.

If you are having trouble quitting smoking, ask your doctor's advice. Programs are available to help you quit as well as prescription drugs.

AN ALABAMA CASE HISTORY

A family I know personally here in Birmingham, Alabama, my home, is a true case history that illustrates the bad effects of smoking. Three brothers and three sisters had the same parents. Only three were smokers. I'll start with the medical problems of the oldest to the youngest.

The oldest is a sister who is now 61 years old. She started smoking when she was 14. By her mid-40s, she was having heart problems. She has had a pacemaker since age 52 and must take blood thinners and heart medication daily.

Her 58-year-old sister started smoking at age 15. In her late 30s, she developed circulation and blood thickening problems. Since her mid-50s, she has had emphysema and heart and artery problems.

The third, a brother, died after two major heart attacks, one at age 44 and another at age 50. He started smoking at age 12. He died of heart failure and lung hemorrhages.

The fourth is a sister, age 51. She is a non-smoker with no major health problems.

The fifth is a brother, age 49. He is also a non-smoker with no health problems. A treadmill test showed only minimal blockage of his arteries.

The last brother, age 45, is a non-smoker. A recent check-up showed he has no health problems.

The three smokers all have had to get false teeth, because smoking restricts the flow of oxygen in the blood vessels to the gums. Judge for yourself. Smoking ruined the health of these people.

If you are a smoker, quit now. Stopping smoking is the best thing you can do for yourself and the ones you love.

LIMIT DRINKING ALCOHOL

Abusing alcohol shrinks brain cells and makes your brain smaller, a recent study in the British Medical Journal has shown. Another study by the National Cancer Institute shows that women who drink three alcoholic drinks a week may increase their risk of breast cancer by as much as fifty percent. Alcohol is also linked to higher risk of rectal, liver and pancreatic cancer.

There are no safe levels of alcohol for women who are pregnant or trying to conceive. Avoid alcohol in pregnancy. Pregnancy requires the highest degree of care in everything the mother puts into her body. Everything she does affects her baby. Alcohol can also limit a man's ability to have sex.

Alcohol is full of calories. Even a couple of beers a day can pile up the calories. But even more cause for concern is the increase in blood pressure with three or more drinks a day. Limit your drinks to one or two a day or week.

One of the biggest problems with alcohol is drinking and driving. Many traffic deaths are caused by drivers who have been drinking. If you drink, don't drive.

If you do abuse alcohol, then seek help. Alcoholics Anonymous has this to say about who is an alcoholic in their pamphlet "Time to Start Living:"

"Whether or not you are an alcoholic is not determined by where you drink, when you started drinking, how long you've been drinking,... what, or even how much. The true test is the answer to this question: What has alcohol done to you? If it has affected your relationships; if it has influenced the way you schedule your days; if it has affected your health,... if you are in any way preoccupied with alcohol — then the likelihood is that you have a problem."

For help with addiction, contact your local United Way office for information on the local Alcoholics Anonymous meetings and other programs. Help is available. Just ask!

FOOD ADDICTION

Many people have found that food is as addictive as alcohol. If the above definition of an alcoholic describes you and food, then you need help.

Overeaters Anonymous was created to help with this problem. Their program helps people — whether they are anorexic or bulimic and underweight or overweight.

The fellowship of others in the OA Program who understand exactly what you are going through helps you to recover and lead a normal, happy healthy life. Call this

"THAT POOR LADY IS STILL BUYING EXPENSIVE DIET FOODS AFTER SUFFERING THROUGH 15 DIFFERENT 'GUARANTEED-TO-LOSE-WEIGHT' DIETS ... AND SHE'S 22 POUNDS HEAVIER NOW THAN WHEN SHE STARTED!"

number for more information: 1-800-743-8703. Meetings are held all across the country.

AIDS

We're all familiar with the terrible illness AIDS (Acquired Immune Deficiency Syndrome), caused by the HIV virus. AIDS is rapidly becoming the No. 1 killer of younger people in the United States, and the epidemic is just beginning.

AIDS attacks and destroys the immune system, leaving the body open to opportunistic deadly infections. Building up and keeping the immune system strong is the best defense for victims and potential victims.

The speedy spread of AIDS has been called an epidemic because it crosses all walks of life. In Alabama alone the number of cases rose by 58 percent between 1990 and 1991. Right now it is incurable. Once a person is infected with the HIV virus, he or she has little chance of avoiding the onset of AIDS — usually in two to five years. Once anyone has an active case of AIDS, the chance of survival is very small.

LEARN AND TEACH PREVENTION

You can do something about AIDS. Take steps to prevent getting AIDS yourself, and teach prevention to your family and friends. Teach responsibility for sexual choices. Keep open the lines of communication about sex with your children. It could mean their lives.

The HIV virus is hard to catch and is not spread by casual contact. Sexual contact and sharing of unclean paraphernalia for intravenous drugs are the most common means of the transmission of the HIV virus.

During sex, HIV is transmitted by contact of bodily fluid (semen, blood, vaginal secretions) with that of an infected person. Always wear condoms for protection. Petroleum jelly interferes with the condom's protection. Ask your pharmacist what lubricant to use.

AIDS is both a heterosexual and a homosexual disease. If you have had more than one sex partner in the last eight years, you should have a test for AIDS, which can be dormant in your body for years.

Blood transfusions have transmitted the disease, but strict steps are now taken to ensure a clean blood supply. If you know you need surgery, you may want to use your own blood by storing it ahead of time.

For more information, call the AIDS hotline, 1-800-342-AIDS.

DON'T GIVE IN TO FEAR

Don't give in to the epidemic of fear that has caused many to cast out friends and family who have AIDS and who, as with any serious illness, need support. You also can offer your help and compassion to local AIDS outreach projects.

We can beat AIDS if:
* we care,
* we don't offer blame — but rather information, and
* we work together with open minds and hearts.
AIDS is a disease, not a moral dilemma.

PROTECT YOUR SKIN FROM THE SUN

Scientists have warned us that the Earth's protective layer of ozone has holes in it, which allows more of the sun's powerful ultraviolet (UV) rays to reach the surface of our planet. Being in the sun without protection is more dangerous than ever before. People are finding they sunburn very quickly.

The sun is responsible for 90 percent of most forms of skin cancer and is also the major cause of wrinkles. If you've ever had a severe or a blistering sunburn, then you are twice as likely to develop skin cancer. Also if you are fair-skinned and burn easily, you are truly at risk.

You need protection from the sun all year. Even in summer, consider wearing long sleeves and pants. Wear lightweight clothing made of tightly woven material. But always wear sunscreen. Big hats like your grandparents wore will help to protect your head and face. Use a sun protection factor (SPF) sunscreen of at least 15, even when the sky is overcast. As much as 85 percent of the harmful rays will come through the clouds. Take care. Also wear sunglasses to protect your retinas and prevent cataracts.

Remember, too, that some commonly used medicines will make your skin more susceptible to the sun's damaging rays. Antibiotics, birth-control pills, estrogen, anti-depressants, diuretics, antihistamines, sedatives and acne medicines all can sensitize your skin. Be informed about the effects of all your medications by asking your doctor or pharmacist about them.

As a precaution, check your body often for signs of skin cancer, especially your back and upper legs. Check for discharge from moles. Pinpoint any moles that have changed shape or size or that look different. See a doctor immediately if you suspect cancer. Skin cancer is treatable in the early stages but can prove fatal.

FAMILY AND CHILDREN PRENATAL CARE

The most important thing a pregnant woman can do for her unborn child is to regularly visit her doctor during the nine months of pregnancy. Premature and underweight babies at birth are the biggest cause of death in children under the age of one.

If the mother smokes or drinks, her baby is more likely to be underweight. Not eating right and being overweight or underweight also can have serious consequences on an unborn child. All parents want a healthy baby, and all babies deserve the healthiest and best start in life.

HAVE FAITH IN **LIFE!** LOVE IT! GET TO KNOW IT...
ENJOY IT! MAKES IT **ALL** WORTH THE EFFORT!

IMMUNIZATION
One of the most important things to remember is to get your children's shots on time. Modern medicine has freed us of many terrible childhood diseases. But if your children don't receive the immunization they need for protection, then they may get a disease and become crippled or die.

BIKE HELMETS
Another crippler and killer of children is sports accidents. If you or your children ride bikes or all-terrain vehicles, be sure everyone wears a helmet every time. Head injuries cause the most deaths in accidents in these kind of sports.

If your kids play a sport, be sure they have the skills to play, are well-supervised and wear the proper safety equipment. A surprising number of little league baseball injuries and even deaths occur each year. These injuries are preventable if parents help out with safety supervision.

CHILD CARE

Parents in many American families work outside the home. I know you want your children well-taken care of either at home or in a child-care facility. The United Way in most cities keeps a list of quality child-care facilities and can send you information on what to look for in good child care.

You and I know a child needs adult supervision until he or she is 12 years old or older. Today many school systems offer supervised, after-school care for school-age children.

Parents need to find or help start good afterschool programs. Homewood, Alabama, has a model program. You can order a book on this subject called Go Ahead, Extend My Day! by Vella and Hollingsworth, 620 Grove Street, Homewood, Alabama 35209.

SCOLIOSIS OR CURVATURE OF THE SPINE

If treated early, most forms of scoliosis or curvature of the spine can be corrected by a chiropractor. The chiropractor uses spinal manipulation to straighten the curve.

Scoliosis, if untreated, can lead to many unhealthy complications and will cause a great deal of pain as a victim gets older. A chiropractor can offer a very simple spinal check of your pre-school child that can detect this serious problem. Then you need to have your child checked regularly because scoliosis can show up later as the child grows.

A CHIROPRACTOR CAN OFFER RELIEF AND HEALING

Chiropractic care is a very effective treatment for all back pain and many other physical problems related to the spine. Almost all trauma to the body affects the spinal column, since the spine is at the center of the body.

Many athletic programs have a chiropractic physician on call to correct the cause of the problem without drugs or surgery. Everybody can benefit from treatment. Using painless and accurate spinal adjustments, the doctor of chiropractic medicine will enhance your body's healing ability, its performance and its resistance to disease.

Scientific data shows chiropractic medicine to be a safe, effective and less expensive means of natural healing. According to statistics, patients of chiropractors are three times more satisfied with their care than patients of family practice physicians.

REMEMBER

o   Quit smoking today because smoking kills.

o   Drink only sparingly since alcohol can be dangerous to your health.

o   Ask for help if you have an alcohol or eating problem.

o   Take good care of your family.

o   Get good medical care during pregnancy.

o   Be sure your children get all their shots.

o   Protect yourself and your family from sports injuries by wearing the right equipment and have proper supervision.

o   Take care in choosing child care.

o   Scoliosis or curvature of the spine can be corrected by a chiropractor if discovered early in childhood.

o   Visit a chiropractor for non-surgical treatment for many problems and to restore your good health.

Chapter 16

THE PROGRAM AND THE FAA

In the introduction of this book, I told you about the problems my bad health caused me with the FAA. The FAA pulled my pilot's license when I was diagnosed with diabetes. One of the requirements I had to meet to get my license back, along with the treadmill and other things, was to go to a certified nutritionist.

I paid a nutritionist $53 an hour to check out the diet I was following. She told me, "Well, Mr. Phillips, this is one of the most perfect diets I have ever seen."

At that time, I had lost over 50 pounds. She said, "But the breakfast on this diet may be giving you too much fruit sugars and not enough protein."

I answered, "Yes, but if you'll notice the six ounces of milk is protein. The oats are 9 percent protein. Because the oats take in the fruit sugar and let it out slowly, I'm not getting a sugar surge. Plus, eating two chicken breasts a day will give me the proper protein, according to the federal government."

After agreeing, she wrote on my card for the FAA that this was the most complete nutritional diet she ever had seen. She found this program to be 100 percent nutritionally right!

I remained on the program and dropped a total of 80 pounds. Today I'm still on the program and feeling great. I have not gained back the weight. You can see from the picture what I looked like when I weighed 230 pounds. I'm lighter today than I've been since I was 12 years old.

Incidentally, I got this nice letter back that stated the United States government was satisfied with my medical record. They gave me back my flying medical and my pilot's license. Now I'm back again as a pilot.

Don't tell me what you don't want to do or what you don't like or this, that or the other. If you want to take that weight off and feel great, follow this program.

You're going to live with this for the rest of your life, which will be longer, healthier and happier because of this change in your lifestyle. This program will help you reach your healthiest, best weight and keep you there.

Remember one thing that's kind of like an old Chinese proverb: If you always do what you've always done, you'll always get what you've always gotten.

Willpower has nothing to do with weight loss. Here's my program. Good luck and good health. Remember, you too can discover the fountain of youth!

Chapter 17

RECOMMENDED READING
AND BIBLIOGRAPHY

I hope you now are interested and excited about taking charge of your health. You can do like I did and learn as much as you can about getting yourself healthy and staying that way.

This list of books and magazines are full of life-changing information. They have helped me to become healthier, and I know they will help you.

FOOD AS MEDICINE

Balch, James E., M.D.; Balch, Phyllis A., C.N.C. Prescription for Nutritional Healing — A Practical A-Z Reference to Drug-Free Remedies Using Vitamins, Minerals, Herbs & Food Supplements. New York, Avery Publishing Group, Inc., 1990.

Carper, Jean, The Food Pharmacy, Dramatic New Evidence That Food Is Your Best Medicine. New York, Bantam Books, 1988.

Cheraskin, M.D., D.M.D., Emanuel and Ringsdorf, Jr., D.M.D., M.S., Marshall with Clark, D.D.S., J. W. Diet And Disease Medical Proof Of Their Life and Death Relationship. Connecticut, Keats Pub., 1987.

Cheraskin, M.D., D.M.D., Emanuel, The Vitamin C Controversy Questions & Answers, Kansas, Bio-Communications Press, 1988.

Cheraskin, M.D., D.M.D., Emanuel and Ringsdorf, Jr., D.M.D., M.S., Marshall, with Dr. Sisley, Emily L., The Vitamin C Connection, New York, Harpers & Row, Pub., 1983.

Cheraskin, M.D., D.M.D., Emanuel, <u>Health And Happiness</u>: Simple, Safe and Sound Systems and Solutions, Kansas, Bio-Communications Press, 1989.

Davis, Adelle, <u>Let's Eat Right To Keep Fit</u>. New York, Harcourt Brace Jovanovich, Inc., 1970.

Dufty, William <u>Sugar Blues</u>. New York: Warner Books, Inc., 1975.

Eades, M.D., Michael R., and Eades, M.D., Mary Dan, <u>Protein Power</u>, New York, Bantam Books, 1996.

Erasmus, Udo, <u>Fats and Oils</u>, The Complete Guide to Fats and Oils in Health and Nutrition. Canada: Alive Books, 1986.

Hausman, Patricia, Hurley, Judith Benn, <u>The Healing Foods</u>, The Ultimate Authority on the Curative Power of Nutrition. Pennsylvania, Rodale Press, 1989.

Hoffman, Jan; Rucker, Chris, <u>The Seventh Day Diet</u>, How The Healthiest People In America Live Better, Longer, Slimmer — And How You Can Too. New York, Canada, Random House, Inc., 1991.

Jensen, Dr. Bernard, <u>Foods That Heal</u>. New York: Avery Publishing Group, Inc., 1988.

Kilham, Christopher S., <u>The Bread & Circus Whole Food Bible</u>. Massachusetts, California, New York: Addison-Wesley Pub., 1991.

Steinman, David, <u>Diet For A Poisoned Planet</u>. How to Choose Safe Foods For You and Your Family. New York: Harmony Books Pub., 1990.

HEART, CHOLESTEROL AND CANCER

Cheraskin, M.D., D.M.D., Emanuel and Oestein, Ph.D., Neil S. with Miner, Paul L., <u>Bio-Nutrionics: Lower Your Cholesterol In 30 Days</u>, New York, Perigee Books-Putnam Pub. Group, 1986.

Cranton, M.D., Elmer and Brecher, Arline, <u>Bypassing Bypass, The New Chelatin Therapy, The Non-Surgical Treatment For Improving Circulation And Slowing the Aging Process</u>. Virginia, Medix Pub., 1984.

Dreher, Henry, Harriet Harvey, <u>Your Defense Against Cancer, The Complete Guide To Cancer Prevention</u>. New York: Harper & Row, Pub., 1988.

Fischer, William L., How To Fight Cancer & Win, Ohio, Fischer Publishing Corporation, 1987.

Harper, M.D., Harold W. and Culbert, Michael L., How You Can Beat The Killer Diseases, New York, Arlington House Pub., 1977.

Natow, Annette B., Heslin, Jo-Ann, The Fat Attack Plan, Your Personal Eating Plan to Get Fat Out of Your Diet for Dramatic Weight Loss, Controlling Cholesterol and a Lifetime of Better Health. New York, Pocket Books, 1990.

DIABETES

Lodewick, M.D., Peter A., A Diabetic Doctor Looks At Diabetes. Massachusetts, R.M.I. Corporation, 1988.

Lowe, Earnest, Arsham, M.D., Ph.D., Gary, Diabetes: A Guide To Living Well, A Program of Individualized Self-Care. Minnesota: Diabetes Center, Inc., 1989.

Steincrohn, M.D., Peter J., Low Blood Sugar, What it is And How to Cure It. New York, Signet, 1972.

EXERCISE AND MORE

Editors of Prevention Magazine Health Books, Everyday Health Tips, 2000 Practical Hints For Better Health And Happiness. Pennsylvania, Rodale Press, 1988.

Hollingsworth, Melinda, Vella, Sandra. Go Ahead, Extend My Day!, Alabama, 1992.

Samford, Ph.D., Bryant A., Shimer, Porter, Fitness Without Exercise, The Scientifically Proven Strategy For Achieving Maximum Health With Minimum Effort. New York: Warner Books, Inc., 1990.

Young, M.D., Stuart H., Dobozin, M.D., Bruce S., Miner, Margaret and the Editors of Consumer Reports Books, Allergies, The Complete Guide To Diagnosis, Treatment, and Daily Management. New York, Consumer Reports Books, 1991.

SEXUAL HEALTH

Comfort, M.B., Ph.D., Alex, editor, The Joy of Sex A Gourmet Guide to Love Making. New York, Simon and Schuster, 1972.

Ortiz, Elizabeth Thompson for Planned Parenthood, Your Complete Guide To Sexual Health. New Jersey, Prentice-Hall, Inc., 1989.

The Boston Women's Health Book Collective, <u>Our Bodies, Ourselves.</u> New York, Simon and Schuster, 1984.

COOKBOOKS

Little, Billie, <u>Recipes For Diabetics</u>, New York, Perigee Books — Putnam Pub., 1981.

Kowalski, Robert E., <u>The 8-Week Cholesterol Cure Cookbook</u>, New York, Harper & Row, 1989.

Shriver, Brenda, Tinsley, Ann. <u>No Red Meat</u>. Arizona: Fisher Books, 1989. (low cholesterol cookbook).

UAB Department of Dietetics, <u>Cookbook for Diabetics and Their Families</u>, Alabama, Oxmoor House, Inc., 1986.

MAGAZINES

<u>Diabetics Forecast</u>, The American Diabetes Association, 1600 Duke Street, Alexandria, VA 22314.

<u>Diabetes Self-Management</u>, P.O. Box 51125, Boulder, CO 80321-1125.

<u>East West NATURAL HEALTH</u>, East West Partners, P.O. Box 57320, Boulder, CO 80322-7320, 1-800-666-8576.

<u>Health</u>, Time Publishing Ventures, Inc., P.O. Box 56863, Boulder, CO 80322-6863, 1-800-274-2522.

TESTIMONY

Dear Archie:

You asked me to give you an evaluation of my health history and activities, and how I managed to have good health, although I'm past the age of 76.

First of all, I inherited a good body. My mother knew a lot about nutrition and saw to it that my brother and I were well-fed. My good health enabled me to follow amateur boxing into my dental college years.

But despite such a good start, I managed to lose my health by the time I was 30 years old. I wasn't aware of nutritional requirements and wasn't interested because at that time I felt I would have good health forever. Or, perhaps I didn't think about it at all, which is a very common attitude.

I, of course, knew that a bad diet was the only cause of dental decay. But since my father and brother were both dentists, I ate what I pleased. I was never taught and had never heard that a bad diet also caused bad health. In fact at that time medical doctors rejected the idea.

My family kept my teeth in good repair, and I still have my natural teeth. However, my health began to fail shortly after I graduated from dental college.

In a few years I had gained 45 pounds over my present weight. I had a large stomach along with frequent head colds and headaches and was allergic to many things. My energy level was low, and I was irritated easily. My nose stayed so congested that I often couldn't breathe except through my mouth. My sinuses were infected at all times, and my disposition was grumpy. The doctors gave me antibiotics of all kinds and were considering a serious operation to open up my sinuses.

About this time, I received in the mail a book written by a dentist, Dr. Melvin E. Page, of St. Petersburg, Florida, from my classmate Dr. John T. Capo in New Orleans. Dr. Page had quit practicing dentistry and was practicing nutrition. The American Medical Association tried everything to stop him including a long, drawn-out lawsuit that Dr. Page won.

This book explained that eating a bad diet such as sugar, white flour, milk, coffee and other processed foods would cause many diseases. It seemed he had written the book for me or at me, because I had most of the problems he predicted. I was so interested I couldn't lay the book down and finished it at 2:00 a.m. This was the first time any doctor or anybody had told me that bad food caused disease.

I immediately quit sugar, white-flour products and milk, including ice cream, all of which I dearly loved. I quit completely. The results were fantastic. Within a month, I could breathe through my nose for the first time in 10 years. I immediately felt better and had a better disposition. In less than a year, I had lost weight down to my fighting trim weight that I still weigh today, 145 pounds.

My marvelous recovery of health after years of medical doctors and their pills by a change in diet made a believer out of me and Dr. Capo. He and I went to St. Petersburg to study under Dr. Page. This started my intensive search for good health and my studying under many health experts.

I returned home from St. Petersburg and started practicing nutrition in addition to doing my dentistry. There was very little money in this, but it satisfied my yearning to help others find their health. In fact I was so eager to help, I ran off a few of my friends. I found out most people did not want to help themselves if it required much study or giving up anything they like.

For years I held public lectures giving free nutritional advice. I continued my own education. I studied under numerous teachers, some in Mexico, Florida, Georgia, California, Chicago, and here in Birmingham, under Drs. Cheraskin and Ringsdorf.

146

I had no trouble helping people get well who would follow the simple instructions. I could fill a book with success stories of people who gained their health where doctors had failed them. But alas, I could fill many more books with stories of sick people who would rather keep the diseases they had than change their life styles. But those who did change their ways and got well made my efforts worthwhile.

Archie, I'm proud that I've influenced you in a small way to becoming so interested in health, first yours, then others, that you've written this book.

The man I bought vitamins from in Milwaukee, Wisconsin, also was a dentist and a famous man in nutritional research at that time. I talked with him about many health matters as well as his experiences with buying, caring for and selling race horses.

He and his wife had a large farm on which they had carefully enriched their pastures and fed and cared for old race horses that no longer could race or be put out to stud. Race horses must win prize money to barely pay for their upkeep. Famous winners make big money with their stud fees, even when they become too old to win races.

He and his wife fed these broken-down horses sprouted grain and gave them vitamins. Although two of the horses died, the others regained their vitality and went back to racing. Several of them beat their own best records. Also they all went back to earning stud fees.

This true story encourages me to believe that there is hope for us old horses yet and hope and direction for young people who want to gain back their health and lose weight.

While Dr. Page's book started me on the search for good health, I did not find it all in one place or at one time. Just what our bodies needed was not clear or easy to determine. There was much false information put out by various interests trying to sell their products.

But despite the misleading propaganda, over the years and piece by piece, the helpful information came in from the many sincere medical researchers. Now you can enjoy a healthy life span in our hostile environment if you're willing to study and learn how to care for your $1 million body. This book will aid you in more easily understanding about good health.

New information is coming in every day. Since we don't know everything about how to be healthy, let's stay alert and do the best we can with what we already know.

Archie, I appreciate the many hours and days you've spent researching this book. I know it is a labor of love and a sincere desire to help others.

I am proud to have helped and delighted to be a party to such a good work.

Sincerely, Klyde Albritton

TABLE 1

National Cholesterol Education Program: Adult Treatment Panel Classification

	Total Cholesterol (mg./dl.)	LDL Cholesterol (mg./dl.)
Desirable	200	130
Borderline high	200-239	130-159
High	240	160

Source: National Cholesterol Education Program, 1988.

Table 2

TWENTY-TWO WAYS TO LOWER CHOLESTEROL

Once a person's blood cholesterol goes above 220 — the generally-accepted level indicating increased susceptibility to heart attack — nutrition-oriented medical doctors usually recommend what comes naturally — using certain foods and vitamin supplements to lower blood cholesterol. Here are natural cholesterol-lowering foods and supplements taken from numerous sources:

1. APPLES eaten on a daily basis have been shown in various studies here and in Europe to lower blood serum cholesterol by approximately 10 percent. Several researchers have put test subjects on two to three apples a day — one in mid-morning and one in mid-afternoon or — in the event of three — one in the early evening.

In an apple-eating experiment by French researcher R. Sable-Amplis, of the University of Paul Sabatier, a group ate two to three apples daily. Eighty percent of the group showed reduced cholesterol within a month — about a 10 percent decline. Good Guy HDL cholesterol rose, and Bad Guy LDL cholesterol dropped.

2. BARLEY is a star at reducing blood-serum cholesterol levels, says Dr. Asaf Qureshi, a scientist in the U.S. Dept. of Agriculture's Cereal Crops Research Unit in Madison, Wisconsin. Dr. Qureshi feels that barley scores by lowering the liver's ability to produce cholesterol. It can be used several times a week as a cooked cereal or in bakery goods — bread or muffins.

3. BEANS (pinto or navy) — as little each day as a cup cooked — lowered cholesterol by 19 percent in subjects tested by Dr. James Anderson, fiber expert at the University of Kentucky. Also the ratio of HDL to LDL became more favorable. (Even baked beans helped, but no sugar, please!)

4. CARROTS (three medium-sized raw, eaten daily) have been shown to lower cholesterol by almost 11 percent.

5. CHILI PEPPER reduces blood-serum cholesterol level by suppressing the liver's ability to produce cholesterol. Researchers in Bangkok, Thailand, made rice-flour noodles, adding two teaspoons of freshly ground jalapeno pepper to slightly more than a cup. Those who

ate the noodles daily experienced lowered cholesterol and increased ability to dissolve blood clots.

6. EGGPLANT serves a special function in cholesterol control, it was discovered at the University of Texas. Eggplant appears to block blood levels of cholesterol from rising when fatty foods have been eaten.

7. GARLIC (a daily ration of five fresh cloves minced into other food) has been shown to lower blood serum cholesterol by nearly 10 percent in 25 days. An Indian researcher, Dr. M. Sucur, fed this amount of garlic to 200 patients. Cholesterol dropped in almost all this group with super-high blood serum levels. After patients reduced their cholesterol to desired levels, Dr. Sucur kept it stable with only two cloves of raw garlic daily.

Another approach: an odorless, socially-acceptable form of garlic sold in health food stores can accomplish the same thing. Scientists at Loma Linda University in California fed four capsules of liquid garlic extract daily to patients with high cholesterol. Six months later, these individuals had achieved an average cholesterol reduction of 44 points.

8. GRAPEFRUIT PECTIN, that gelatinous stuff that holds jelly together, can lower cholesterol. Dr. James Cerda, a researcher at the University of Florida, fed patients with high cholesterol a little more than 1/2-ounce of grapefruit pectin capsules daily and, in four months, brought their cholesterol down by an average of 8 percent. (Most health food stores carry this supplement).

9. LECITHIN derived from soybeans — slightly more than an ounce daily — reduced blood levels of cholesterol by 18 percent.

10. MILK (skim) lowers cholesterol, as demonstrated by several researchers.

11. OAT BRAN, a water-soluble fiber, is one the most effective foods for reducing cholesterol. A study by Dr. J.W. Anderson revealed that eating oat bran daily as a cereal or in muffin form can reduce blood cholesterol by up to 19 percent.

12. OLIVE OIL, as demonstrated by Dr. Scott M. Grundy, of the Center for Human Nutrition at the University of Texas in Dallas,

can lower or control cholesterol levels. Grundy keeps his blood cholesterol in line by taking two teaspoonsful daily and holds his consumption of fats to between 30 and 35 percent of total calories.

13. ONIONS have scored high in a number of studies for reducing cholesterol levels in human beings and animals, with high grades for raising the beneficial (HDL) over the harmful variety, LDL.

14. PLANTAINS (LARGE GREEN BANANAS) — one half to a whole unit daily — have been discovered to lower blood cholesterol dramatically and create a more favorable ratio between HDL and LDL cholesterol. Ripe plantains don't work. (Green plantains are available in many supermarkets and in produce stores).

15. SEAFOOD eaten several times a week contributes to controlling fat circulating in the blood and keeping cholesterol levels from elevating, indicate many studies.

16. SEAWEED such as kelp lowers cholesterol in a manner that researchers can't quite fathom. It seems to remove cholesterol from the intestine. (If you're not into eating seaweed, Japanese-style, you might want kelp tablets from the health food store).

17. SOYBEANS and products derived from them — soy milk, lecithin and tofu — help break down fatty deposits so that they can be flushed from the body more readily — and, in the process, also lower blood cholesterol. Soybean products seem to work best on patients with extra-high cholesterol, 300 or more. Researchers at the University of Milan, Italy, caused cholesterol levels to plummet by 15 to 20 percent, simply by having patients eat soybeans used in various recipes in place of meat and milk products.

18. SPINACH proved a good cholesterol-reducer in animal experiments by Japanese scientists.

19. YAMS (SWEET POTATOES), which contain much water-soluble fiber in addition to beta-carotene, contribute to cholesterol control, if eaten four or five times weekly. In a Japanese experiment, sweet potato fiber proved the best of 28 fruit and vegetable fibers for binding with cholesterol and removing it.

20. YOGURT is a real winner in lowering cholesterol. Three cups a day have caused cholesterol levels to decline by as much as five percent a week, with the proportion of Good Guy HDL rising in ratio to LDL.

21. VITAMIN C has been shown in experiments by England's Constance Spittle Leslie, a pathologist at Pinderfields Hospital in Wakefield, Yorkshire, in units of 1,000 mg daily to decrease her blood cholesterol from 230 to 140. When she discontinued taking this vitamin, her cholesterol returned to its former level. Patients at the hospital experienced a similar reduction on her vitamin C regime.

22. DAILY VIGOROUS EXERCISE has been shown by researcher Josef Patsch, at Baylor College of Medicine in Texas to increase the ratio of HDL to LDL and rid the blood of excessive fats. But according to Patsch, the benefits won't last forever, and the program must be continued regularly.

TABLE 3

SOURCES OF LINOLEIC ACID

Safflower oil
Corn oil
Cottonseed oil
Soybean oil
Sesame oil
Black walnuts
English walnuts
Sunflower seeds
Brazil nuts
Margarine
Pumpkin and squash seeds
Spanish peanuts
Peanut butter
Almonds

TABLE 4

TYPES OF FATS ACCORDING TO SATURATION

Type	% Poly-Unsaturated	% Mono-Unsaturated	% Saturated
Mostly Polyunsaturated			
Corn oil	62	25	13
Cottonseed oil	54	19	27
Safflower oil	78	13	9
Soybean oil	61	24	15
Sunflower oil	69	20	11
Mostly Monounsaturated			
Canola oil	31	62	7
Margarine, hard	29	35-66	17-25
Margarine, soft	61	14-36	10-17
Margarine, tub	46	22-48	15-23
Olive oil	9	77	14
Peanut oil	34	48	18
Sesame seed oil	44	41	15
Vegetable shortening (e.g., Crisco)	33	41-55	22-33
Mostly Saturated			
Beef fat	4	44	52
Butter	4	30	66
Coconut oil	2	6	92
Palm oil	10	39	51
Palm kernel	2	12	86

Source: U.S. Department of Agriculture

TABLE 5

TIPS ON LOW-FAT COOKING AND SHOPPING

1. Choose lean cuts of meat and trim fat before cooking.

2. Roast, bake, broil, or simmer meat, poultry, and fish. Cook meat or poultry on a rack so that the fat will drain off.

3. Remove the skin from poultry before cooking. Avoid pre-basted turkey, which is often injected with saturated coconut oil.

4. Chill meat or poultry broth, stews, and soups until the fat rises to the top, and can be spooned off.

5. Sear meat quickly in a nonstick pan and then lower the heat to cook to desired doneness; if heated slowly, the meat will cook in its own fats. Vegetables absorb fat and therefore should never be browned with meat.

6. Nonstick cookware and nonstick vegetable cooking sprays reduce the need for oil and shortening.

7. Most salad dressings are high in fats and calories. Use fat-free or low-fat preparations or lemon juice; low-fat yogurt or cottage cheese whipped in a blender makes an acceptable dressing.

8. A blender or food processor can be used to whip cold water with butter or margarine to produce a product lower in calories per tablespoon measure.

9. Allow butter or margarine to soften before use, so that it can be spread thinly.

10. Do not add oil to pasta water; butter or margarine to rice; butter or milk to mashed potatoes. The pasta does not need it. Instead, flavor rice with parsley, onion, herbs, or spices; add low-fat yogurt or buttermilk to the potatoes.

11. Replace whole milk with low-fat or skim milk in all recipes. Evaporated skim milk can be whipped in a chilled mixing bowl and is a good substitute in dishes requiring cream.

12. Avoid nondairy creamers and nondairy toppings, which are usually high in saturated fats (palm or coconut oils) and calories.

13. Reduce your intake of regular mayonnaise, which has 100 calories per tablespoon. Select low-fat brands or mix with an equal amount of low-fat yogurt to make a dressing for things such as potato salad. Use mustard in sandwiches.

14. Saute vegetables in chicken stock, bouillon, or wine instead of in butter, margarine, or oil.

15. Serve smaller portions of high-fat foods, while increasing portion sizes of pasta, vegetables, fruit, and other low-fat items.

16. When shopping, look for the low-fat or reduced calorie varieties of yogurt, cottage cheese, and processed foods.

17. Use low-fat plain yogurt, buttermilk, or low-fat cottage cheese instead of sour cream in dips or for baking. Adding a little cornstarch when cooking will prevent curdling.

18. In most recipes, the fat or oil can be reduced by a third without altering texture or taste.

TABLE 6

FAT CONTENT OF COMMON FOODS
BY PERCENT OF CALORIES

	Fat Calories/%	Protein Calories/%	Carbohydrates Calories/%	Total Calories/%
90 to 100% Fat				
Italian Dressing (1 T)	72/94	0/0	5/6	77
Lard (1 T)	126/100	0/0	0/0	126
Vegetable Oil (Crisco)	122/100	0/0	0/0	122
Beef tallow (1 oz)	252/100	0/0	0/0	252
Butter (1 T)	108/100	0/0	0/0	108
Margarine (1 T)	108/100	0/0	0/0	108
Mayonnaise (1 T)	99/98	1/1	1/1	101
Bacon/Fried Crisp (1 strip)	45/92	4/8	0/0	49